Fail Forward

Turning Missteps Into Mastery

By

W.J. Simpson

Copyright © 2025 by W. J. Simpson

All Rights Reserved

No part of this book may be reprinted or reproduced, or utilized in any form or by any electronic, mechanical, or other means now known or hereafter invented, including photocopying and recording, or in any information storage or retrieval system, without permission in writing from the publisher.

Table of Contents

Introduction 1

Chapter 1: The Fear of Falling 2

Chapter 2: Redefining Failure 6

Chapter 3: The Anatomy of Mistakes 11

Chapter 4: Failing to Succeed 17

Chapter 5: The Shame Spiral 22

Chapter 6: Facing Criticism with Courage 27

Chapter 7: The Grit to Persist 32

Chapter 8: From Regret to Redemption 37

Chapter 9: Losing Them 43

Chapter 10: Iterative Improvement 46

Chapter 11: Married Too Soon 52

Chapter 12: The Role of Mentors and Allies 57

Chapter 13: When Failure Leads to Innovation 63

Chapter 14: Failing as a Leader 69

Chapter 15: The Risk-Reward Equation 75

Chapter 16: Making Peace with Imperfection 81

Chapter 17: The Spirit of a Conqueror 85

Chapter 18: A New Kind of Hope 87

Chapter 19: Teaching Others to Fail Forward 91

Chapter 20: The Sweet Spot of Success 97

Chapter 21: Helping Hands, Healing Hearts 103

Chapter 22: Failing in Relationships and Life 107

Chapter 23: The Fail-Forward Mindset.................................. 113

Chapter 24: The Road to Redemption 118

Chapter 25: When You've Hit Rock Bottom 122

Chapter 26: From Misstep to Mastery.................................. 127

Chapter 27: The Fail-Forward Framework........................... 129

Chapter 28: Your Fail-Forward Legacy 135

About the Author.. 138

Introduction

Fail Forward: Turning Missteps into Mastery is a transformative guide that flips the script on failure. This book is not just about overcoming fear—it's about embracing failure as a vital part of the journey toward greatness. Using vivid storytelling, actionable strategies, and profound insights, it takes readers on a journey through the moments that often paralyze us, showing how those very moments can become the catalysts for growth, resilience, and eventual mastery.

Imagine turning every misstep into a stepping stone, every setback into a setup for success. From navigating self-doubt to reframing perceived defeats, Fail Forward equips readers with tools to rewire their mindset, conquer hesitation, and boldly take the leaps that lead to greatness. It's a book for dreamers, doers, and anyone ready to transform their fear of falling into the courage to soar.

This is your permission slip to fail—and to discover that failure is not the end, but the beginning of extraordinary growth. Ready to leap? Fail Forward will show you how.

Chapter 1:
The Fear of Falling

Imagine standing on the edge of a diving board, high above the water. Your legs shake as you glance down, a mix of curiosity and dread swirling inside you. The distance looks immense, the water below uninviting. You've seen others leap, their laughter echoing as they surface unscathed. But for you, the fear is paralyzing. What if you belly flop? What if you don't surface as gracefully as others? What if you fail?

This hesitation, this internal resistance, is the fear of falling—a universal experience rooted deep in our psyche. It's not just about a physical leap but about emotional and psychological risks that hold us back from achieving our potential. To move forward, we must understand this fear and learn to navigate it.

Where the Fear Comes From

The fear of failure is ancient, hardwired into our biology. Our ancestors' survival often depended on avoiding mistakes. A wrong step could mean injury, starvation, or death. Over time, this survival instinct evolved into a more complex fear—one that isn't just about physical danger but also about social rejection, embarrassment, and self-doubt.

Modern life amplifies these fears. From an early age, we're conditioned to strive for perfection. Gold stars, good grades, promotions—our achievements become synonymous with our worth. Failure, meanwhile, is stigmatized. It's seen as a blemish on our record rather than a natural step in the learning process. This creates a culture of fear, where taking risks feels like gambling with our self-esteem.

How Fear Holds Us Back

The fear of failure doesn't just stop us from trying new things—it corrodes our confidence, limits our creativity, and keeps us stuck in our comfort zones.

1. Paralysis Through Perfectionism: Many people hesitate to act unless they're sure they'll succeed. This mindset leads to procrastination and missed opportunities. The pursuit of perfection becomes a trap, convincing us that doing nothing is safer than doing something imperfectly.

2. Avoiding the Unknown: Fear convinces us to play it safe. We avoid new challenges, declining promotions, turning down opportunities, or never starting the business we dream about. It whispers, What if you're not good enough?

3. Defining Failure Too Narrowly: Too often, we define success and failure in rigid terms. If we don't achieve exactly what we set out to do, we label the experience a failure, ignoring the lessons and growth that came from trying.

The Hidden Costs of Fear

Ironically, the fear of failure often leads to the very thing we're trying to avoid: stagnation and regret. A life spent avoiding risks is one where potential goes untapped.

Imagine what Thomas Edison's life would have looked like if he had stopped after his first failed experiment. Or J.K. Rowling if she had let rejection letters define her future. Both of these individuals faced monumental failures—but they didn't let fear win.

The cost of not trying is often greater than the pain of failing. Regret is a heavier burden than mistakes.

Reframing Fear

The key to overcoming the fear of failure is not to eliminate it but to change how we see it. Fear is not the enemy; it's a sign that you're stepping into something meaningful. Here's how to reframe your relationship with failure:

1. Separate Fear From Fact: Fear often exaggerates the consequences of failure. Challenge your inner dialogue. Ask yourself, What's the worst that could happen? You'll likely find that the stakes aren't as high as your fear makes them seem.

2. Focus on the Process, Not the Outcome: Shift your goal from "succeeding" to "learning." Every attempt is a step forward, regardless of the result.

3. Celebrate Your Courage: The act of trying—regardless of the outcome—is a victory in itself. Every step outside your comfort zone builds resilience and prepares you for future challenges.

A Leap Worth Taking

The truth is, the fear of falling never completely goes away. Even seasoned entrepreneurs, artists, and leaders feel it when they embark on something new. What sets them apart is their willingness to jump anyway.

The next time you stand on that metaphorical diving board, remember: the water below isn't as scary as it seems. Take the leap. If you fall, you'll learn how to rise. And each rise brings you closer to the mastery you seek.

The fear of falling is only the beginning of your journey—if you let it be.

Reflection Question:

What is one risk you've avoided due to fear? How might your life be different if you embraced it instead?

Chapter 2:
Redefining Failure

Failure. Just the word itself stirs an ache in the chest, doesn't it? It carries weight, shame, disappointment. From childhood, we're taught to avoid it at all costs, to see it as a final verdict on our abilities and our worth. But what if failure isn't an ending? What if it's not a wall but a doorway—a path that, though painful, leads to wisdom, strength, and success?

To achieve anything meaningful in life, we must redefine failure. We must see it not as a cruel judge, but as a relentless teacher.

Failure Is Not the Opposite of Success

The first step in redefining failure is understanding that it isn't the antithesis of success—it's part of the journey toward it. Consider this: every great invention, every monumental achievement, every life-changing discovery was born out of failure.

Thomas Edison, when asked about the thousands of failed attempts before he invented the light bulb, replied,

"I have not failed. I've just found 10,000 ways that won't work."

Let that sink in for a moment. Edison didn't see failure as a stop sign. He saw it as a roadmap—each misstep pointing him closer to the right answer. What if you started seeing your own failures the same way?

The Stories We Tell Ourselves

So much of how we perceive failure is rooted in the stories we tell ourselves. When we fail, we tend to attach meaning to it:

- "I'm not good enough."
- "I'll never succeed."
- "This isn't meant for me."

But failure doesn't define you. It's not a reflection of your worth; it's simply an event, a moment in time. You failed at something—you are not a failure.

Dr. Carol Dweck, the psychologist behind the concept of the growth mindset, writes,

"In a growth mindset, failure is not a verdict—it's a beginning."

What if, instead of seeing failure as proof of inadequacy, you saw it as evidence that you're trying? That you're brave enough to take risks? That you're growing?

Rewriting Failure's Narrative

Think back to a time when you failed. Maybe it was a project that didn't turn out as planned. A relationship that ended in heartbreak. A goal you didn't achieve. Now ask yourself: What did I learn from that experience? How did it shape me?

Here's the truth: failure often teaches us more than success ever could. Success feels good, but it doesn't demand introspection. Failure forces us to look inward. It humbles us. It sharpens our focus.

In the words of Maya Angelou:

"You may encounter many defeats, but you must not be defeated. In fact, it may be necessary to encounter defeats so you can know who you are, what you can rise from, how you can still come out of it."

Failure is the furnace that forges resilience. It strips away ego and leaves behind the raw, unbreakable core of who you are.

Learning to Fail Well

Redefining failure doesn't mean you won't feel the sting when things go wrong. It doesn't mean you'll never cry or question yourself. What it means is that you'll learn to fail well.

To fail well is to:

1. Accept the Lesson: Ask yourself, What did this teach me? Every failure has a lesson, if you're willing to look for it.
2. Detach From Perfection: Stop demanding perfection of yourself. It's an impossible standard that stifles growth. Instead, aim for progress, not perfection.
3. Stay in the Game: Don't let failure knock you out. Get back up. Keep moving forward. Remember, success isn't about never falling—it's about always rising.

Nelson Mandela put it best:

"I never lose. I either win or learn."

What if you adopted that mindset? What if you saw every failure as a step forward rather than a step back?

The Courage to Fail

It takes immense courage to embrace failure. It's not easy to put yourself out there, to risk rejection or ridicule. But think about this: what's the alternative? A life spent playing it safe? A life where you never risk failure but also never taste the sweetness of achievement?

Brené Brown, a researcher on courage and vulnerability, writes:

"There is no innovation and creativity without failure. Period."

The choice is clear. To do anything worthwhile, you must risk failure. To live a life of meaning, you must be willing to fall—and then rise again.

Turning Pain into Power

One of the most powerful aspects of redefining failure is learning to transform its pain into purpose. J.K. Rowling, before she became one of the most successful authors in history, described herself as "the biggest failure I knew." Rejected by multiple publishers, she could have given up. Instead, she let failure strip away everything unimportant in her life. It clarified her vision and strengthened her resolve.

"It is impossible to live without failing at something," Rowling said, "unless you live so cautiously that you might as well not have lived at all—in which case, you fail by default."

Let that truth sink in. The pain of failure pales in comparison to the regret of never trying.

A New Definition

By the end of this chapter, I want you to write your own definition of failure. Not the one society has taught you, but one that empowers you. Here's mine:

Failure is the process of becoming.

When you fail, you are in motion. You are learning, growing, evolving. You are shedding old limitations and stepping into a stronger version of yourself.

So, the next time failure finds you—and it will—don't hide from it. Don't shrink. Instead, look it in the eye and say, "Thank you for the lesson. I'm ready to rise."

Reflection Question:

What failure in your life taught you the most? How did it shape the person you are today?

Chapter 3:
The Anatomy of Mistakes

Mistakes are life's way of getting our attention. They force us to pause, reflect, and often change course. While no one enjoys making them, mistakes are not random misfortunes. They are the result of specific patterns, decisions, and circumstances. To grow, we must understand why mistakes happen, dissect them without judgment, and learn how to use them as stepping stones toward progress.

If failure is the teacher, then mistakes are the lessons. Let's break them down.

Why Do We Make Mistakes?

Mistakes often stem from one of three root causes:

1. Lack of Knowledge: We're trying something new, and we don't yet have the skills or experience to get it right.

2. External Pressures: Stress, deadlines, or distractions push us to act quickly or without full clarity.

3. Human Fallibility: We are not perfect beings. Our emotions, biases, and limitations sometimes lead us astray.

Recognizing these causes is key. When you understand why you made a mistake, you can address the root issue rather than just its symptoms.

The Danger of Ignoring Mistakes

The real risk isn't making a mistake—it's failing to learn from it. Mistakes that go unexamined tend to repeat themselves. As philosopher George Santayana famously said:

"Those who cannot remember the past are condemned to repeat it."

By ignoring mistakes, we not only miss out on valuable lessons but also allow shame and denial to fester. Over time, this can lead to stagnation, missed opportunities, and even larger failures.

The key is to see mistakes not as indictments of your character but as invitations to grow.

The Mistake Cycle

Most mistakes follow a predictable cycle:

1. The Trigger: A decision, action, or assumption sets the stage for the mistake. This could be a moment of impulsivity, a miscalculation, or an unchecked emotion.
2. The Fallout: The consequences become apparent—an error at work, a hurtful comment in a relationship, or a missed goal.
3. The Response: You either react defensively, ignore it, or confront it head-on.
4. The Lesson: If you analyze the mistake, you extract its wisdom. If you don't, the cycle repeats.

Breaking free from this cycle requires conscious effort and self-awareness.

How to Analyze a Mistake for Growth

When you make a mistake, the natural reaction is to feel embarrassment, frustration, or regret. But instead of getting stuck in those emotions, use them as fuel for reflection. Here's how:

1. Pause and Reflect:

Before rushing to fix the mistake, pause. Acknowledge what happened without judgment. Ask yourself:

- What were the circumstances leading up to this mistake?
- Was this a result of my actions, or were there external factors involved?

2. Separate the Mistake from Your Identity:

You are not your mistakes. Instead of saying, "I'm a failure," reframe it: "I made a mistake." This shift allows you to focus on the action rather than internalizing blame.

3. Ask the Right Questions:

- What specifically went wrong?
- Was there a decision I could have made differently?
- What assumptions or biases influenced my actions?

4. Identify the Lesson:

Every mistake has something to teach. Maybe you need to communicate more clearly, double-check your work, or slow down in high-pressure situations. Write down the lesson—literally. Studies show that writing helps solidify learning.

5. Make a Plan:

Apply what you've learned. What will you do differently next time? Create specific, actionable steps to prevent the mistake from happening again.

When Mistakes Hurt

Some mistakes leave scars—relationships damaged, opportunities lost, trust broken. These mistakes are the hardest to face, but they also offer the deepest growth.

Take responsibility for your actions, and where possible, make amends. Apologies can't erase the past, but they can pave the way for healing. More importantly, forgive yourself. As Lewis B. Smedes wrote:

"To forgive is to set a prisoner free and discover that the prisoner was you."

Even when mistakes hurt, they can lead to transformation. The pain you feel today may be the catalyst for a stronger, wiser version of yourself tomorrow.

The Hidden Benefits of Mistakes

It may sound strange, but mistakes have benefits:

1. They Build Resilience: Each time you recover from a mistake, you strengthen your ability to face future challenges.
2. They Foster Innovation: Many of the world's greatest discoveries were mistakes. Penicillin, Post-it notes, and even chocolate chip cookies were born from errors.
3. They Inspire Empathy: Making mistakes reminds us of our shared humanity. It humbles us and helps us connect with others.

As Albert Einstein said,

"Anyone who has never made a mistake has never tried anything new."

When you embrace your mistakes, you open yourself to a life of curiosity, creativity, and growth.

A Mistake is a Mirror

Mistakes are not enemies. They are mirrors, reflecting back areas where we need to grow. When you make a mistake, it's not the universe punishing you—it's life showing you where to improve.

Instead of fearing mistakes, welcome them. Ask yourself: What is this mistake here to teach me? How can I use it to become better, stronger, wiser?

Redemption Through Growth

To err is human, but to grow from those errors is transformative. The Japanese art of kintsugi—repairing broken pottery with gold—offers a profound metaphor for life. Instead of hiding the cracks, kintsugi highlights them, turning the object into something more beautiful than before.

You, too, can embrace your mistakes, filling the cracks with the gold of wisdom and resilience.

Closing Thought

Mistakes are not the end of the road—they are signposts along the way. They guide us, shape us, and ultimately lead us closer to the person we're meant to become.

As you move forward, remember this:

"Our greatest glory is not in never falling, but in rising every time we fall." – Confucius

Mistakes are inevitable. Growth is optional. Choose growth.

Reflection Question:

What is one mistake you've made recently? What lesson did it teach you, and how will you apply it moving forward?

Chapter 4:
Failing to Succeed

Failure has a way of stripping us bare. It forces us to confront the raw, unfiltered truth of who we are and where we stand. But the truth about failure is this: it isn't the end. In fact, it's often the beginning of something extraordinary. Some of the most iconic individuals in history achieved greatness not despite their failures but because of them. Their stories remind us that failure, no matter how devastating, is often the foundation for success.

This chapter is not just about their stories; it's about mine—and perhaps yours too. It's about falling so hard you think you'll never rise, only to find that the very act of rising transforms you.

The Stories That Inspire

History is filled with tales of people who faced immense setbacks before achieving monumental success:

- Walt Disney was fired from a newspaper job because he "lacked imagination and had no good ideas." Yet from that failure grew a dream that brought magic to millions.
- Oprah Winfrey, now a media mogul, was told she was "unfit for television" and fired from her first anchor position. She took that rejection and built a platform to change lives.
- Michael Jordan, widely regarded as the greatest basketball player of all time, once said, "I've missed more than 9,000 shots in my career. I've lost almost 300 games. On 26 occasions, I've been trusted to take the game-winning shot

and missed. I've failed over and over and over again in my life. And that is why I succeed."

These stories are more than inspiring—they're proof that failure doesn't define us. What defines us is how we respond to it.

When Failure Felt Like the End: My Story

For me, failure wasn't a single event—it came in waves, relentless and unyielding. Each one knocked me down harder than the last.

I remember the night I was arrested like it was yesterday. The cold metal of the handcuffs, the piercing sting of humiliation, and the sinking realization that I had hit rock bottom. Sitting in that cell, I wasn't thinking about redemption. I was drowning in shame, convinced that my life would forever be defined by that moment.

Not long after, I lost my grandparents—my lifelines, my anchors. They were the ones who always saw the best in me, even when I couldn't see it myself. Their absence left a gaping hole in my heart, and I spiraled deeper into despair.

And then came the divorce. The failure of my marriage felt like the final blow. I carried the weight of self-blame, wondering if I was too broken to deserve love.

It was during this time, at my lowest point, that I sat in the darkness of my depression and cried out to God. I felt completely shattered, but I was reminded of a powerful verse:

"The Lord is close to the brokenhearted and saves those who are crushed in spirit." – Psalm 34:18

God didn't take away the pain, but He gave me the strength to face it. Piece by piece, I began to rebuild.

The Turning Point: Finding the Lesson in Failure

What I learned during those years was that failure isn't a life sentence—it's a life lesson. Each loss, each mistake, each heartbreak carried a hidden gift, though it took time to see it.

- My arrest taught me humility. It forced me to confront the choices I had made and commit to doing better. It became the wake-up call I didn't know I needed.
- Losing my grandparents taught me resilience. Their love gave me a foundation that even death couldn't take away. I carry their wisdom with me every day.
- Divorce taught me self-love. It made me realize that my worth isn't dependent on someone else's validation. I had to learn to love myself first before I could truly love others.

Through it all, I discovered that failure wasn't breaking me—it was shaping me.

How God Turned My Pain into Purpose

When I was in the depths of my despair, I couldn't see how any of it could lead to success. But God had a plan.

I started small, focusing on one step at a time. I leaned into my faith, trusted the process, and began to see opportunities where I once saw only obstacles. Slowly, my failures became the foundation for something greater.

"And we know that in all things God works for the good of those who love him, who have been called according to his purpose." – Romans 8:28

This verse became my lifeline. It reminded me that my failures weren't wasted. They were part of a divine blueprint, one that would lead me to my purpose.

The Stories That Connect Us

My story isn't unique, but it's personal. It's a testament to the fact that failure doesn't discriminate—it touches all of us. But so does redemption.

When I think of others who turned their pain into purpose, I'm reminded of Steve Jobs, who was fired from Apple, the company he co-founded. He later said, "Getting fired from Apple was the best thing that could have ever happened to me. It freed me to enter one of the most creative periods of my life."

And then there's Nelson Mandela, who spent 27 years in prison, only to emerge as a symbol of hope and forgiveness. As he so eloquently put it:

"Do not judge me by my successes, judge me by how many times I fell down and got back up again."

These stories connect us because they remind us that failure isn't final. It's a stepping stone, not a tombstone.

Failing Forward

Failing to succeed isn't about avoiding failure—it's about embracing it. It's about understanding that every misstep, every heartbreak, every loss is part of a bigger story.

When I look back now, I don't see a series of failures. I see a series of lessons that led me here.

If you're in the middle of your own storm, take heart. You are not defined by your failures. You are defined by your resilience, your courage, and your faith. As the poet Rumi once wrote:

"Don't grieve. Anything you lose comes round in another form."

Reflection Question

What failure in your life felt like the end, but turned out to be the beginning of something greater?

Your success story is still being written. Keep going. Keep failing. Keep succeeding.

Chapter 5:
The Shame Spiral

Failure has a way of sticking to you, not just as an event but as a label. The shame that follows can be overwhelming, spiraling into self-doubt, embarrassment, and isolation. It whispers lies into your soul: "You'll never recover from this. Everyone knows you're a fraud. You're not enough."

This is the shame spiral—a vicious cycle that traps you in a loop of self-condemnation and inaction. But here's the truth: shame doesn't have to be the end of your story. It's not easy to break free, but it's possible. I know because I've been there, drowning in my own shame, and I found a way out.

Understanding the Spiral

Shame begins with a mistake—a decision gone wrong, a plan that failed, or a moment of weakness exposed. It's not the mistake itself that causes the spiral, though—it's how we internalize it.

- Guilt says, "I made a mistake."
- Shame says, "I am the mistake."

This difference is critical. Guilt can motivate change, but shame paralyzes us. It isolates us from others, convincing us that we're unworthy of love, forgiveness, or redemption.

Psychologist Carl Jung once wrote, "Shame is a soul-eating emotion." It consumes you from the inside out, making it difficult to move forward.

The Signs You're in a Shame Spiral

1. Negative Self-Talk: You replay the mistake in your mind, calling yourself names like "stupid," "failure," or "worthless."

2. Avoidance: You avoid people, situations, or opportunities that remind you of the failure.

3. Emotional Paralysis: You feel stuck, unable to take action or make decisions for fear of making another mistake.

4. Self-Sabotage: Believing you're unworthy of success, you might subconsciously ruin chances for progress.

If you've experienced these feelings, know this: you are not alone. Shame affects everyone at some point, but it doesn't have to control your future.

The Night Shame Took Over

I'll never forget the moment I realized I was trapped in the shame spiral. It was after my arrest, a night that changed everything. I remember sitting alone, my head in my hands, consumed by a mix of embarrassment and regret.

The whispers of shame were relentless:

- "What kind of person does this?"
- "You've ruined your life."
- "Your family will never look at you the same."

The shame wasn't just about the mistake—it was about who I thought I was because of it. I believed I was broken beyond repair.

Things only worsened after my divorce. I felt like a public failure, exposed for the world to see. I isolated myself, convinced that no one could understand what I was going through. The weight of shame was suffocating, and I couldn't see a way out.

Breaking Free from Shame

The turning point didn't come overnight. It came in small, deliberate steps, fueled by a deep desire to stop letting shame dictate my life. Here's what helped me escape the spiral:

1. Naming the Shame

Shame thrives in secrecy. The first step to breaking free is acknowledging it. I had to face the truth: I was ashamed of my choices, but I couldn't let them define me.

I wrote down my thoughts, pouring out every painful emotion onto the page. Seeing the words in black and white helped me separate the feelings from myself.

2. Challenging the Lies

Shame tells us lies about our worth. I started asking myself, "Is this true? Am I really worthless because of this mistake?" Slowly, I began replacing those lies with truths:

- "I made a mistake, but I am still valuable."
- "This moment doesn't define my entire life."

A quote that stayed with me during this time was from Maya Angelou:

"I can be changed by what happens to me. But I refuse to be reduced by it."

3. Talking to Someone I Trusted

Shame can't survive empathy. When I finally opened up to a trusted friend about what I was going through, I felt an immediate sense of relief. They didn't judge me—they listened.

Sharing my story didn't erase the shame, but it loosened its grip.

4. Practicing Self-Compassion

I realized that I was harder on myself than I would ever be on someone else. If a friend had made the same mistakes, I wouldn't have condemned them—I would have encouraged them to learn and grow.

So, I started treating myself with the same kindness. I forgave myself, not because I deserved it, but because I needed it to move forward.

5. Reframing Failure as Growth

My mistakes weren't the end of my story—they were lessons. The arrest, the divorce, the brokenness—they taught me resilience, humility, and the importance of leaning on my faith.

I began to see failure as a stepping stone rather than a stumbling block. As Thomas Edison said after countless failed experiments:

"I have not failed. I've just found 10,000 ways that won't work."

How Faith Helped Me Heal

During my darkest moments, I turned to God. I remember crying out, desperate for guidance and hope. I came across this verse:

"Those who look to him are radiant; their faces are never covered with shame." – Psalm 34:5

It reminded me that God doesn't see us through the lens of our mistakes. He sees us as His children, worthy of love and redemption.

Faith became my anchor. It reminded me that my failures weren't wasted—they were part of a bigger plan.

The Road to Redemption

Breaking free from the shame spiral isn't a one-time event. It's a journey—a series of choices to rise above self-doubt and embrace growth.

- Step by step, I rebuilt my confidence.
- Moment by moment, I chose courage over fear.
- Day by day, I learned to see myself not as a failure but as someone who failed and got back up.

I'm not perfect, and I still have moments of self-doubt. But shame no longer controls me. I've learned to let go of the weight I was never meant to carry.

A New Narrative

If you're trapped in the shame spiral, know this: you are not your mistakes. You are not defined by your failures. You are more resilient, more capable, and more loved than you realize.

As Brené Brown wisely said:

"Shame corrodes the very part of us that believes we are capable of change."

You are capable of change. You are worthy of redemption. And your story isn't over—it's just beginning.

Reflection Question:

What mistake are you holding onto that no longer serves you? How can you start breaking free from the shame spiral today?

Chapter 6:
Facing Criticism with Courage

Criticism. It's the thing we dread more than bad Wi-Fi, awkward small talk, or showing up to a party an hour too early. Whether it comes from a well-meaning friend, a blunt coworker, or that one family member who seems to think "constructive" is just another word for "cruel," criticism can hit like a gut punch. But here's the twist: criticism, when handled correctly, isn't a weapon—it's a tool.

Learning to face criticism with courage doesn't just help you grow; it also helps you laugh at the absurdity of how seriously we sometimes take ourselves. Trust me—I've had to learn this the hard way, and some of the lessons are as hilarious as they are heart-touching.

My First Real Encounter with Criticism

Let me take you back to my first big moment of criticism. Picture this: me, standing confidently in the middle of a middle school talent show, belting out an almost recognizable rendition of Whitney Houston's "I Will Always Love You." I say "almost" because, halfway through, my voice cracked so loudly a kid in the back yelled, "Is that a dog?"

The audience laughed. My confidence shattered like a dropped iPhone without a case.

As I walked off the stage, a teacher patted me on the back and said, "Well, that was brave!" Brave? Was that code for "terrible"? At the time, it felt like a dagger to the heart. But looking back, it was one of my first lessons in handling criticism: sometimes it's not about what people say but how you interpret it.

Why Criticism Hurts (and Why It's Okay)

Criticism stings because it pokes at our insecurities. We all want to feel capable, smart, and appreciated, and when someone points out our flaws, it feels like they're questioning our worth. But here's the kicker: criticism isn't always an attack. Sometimes, it's a mirror showing us something we couldn't see on our own.

As Aristotle famously said, "There is only one way to avoid criticism: do nothing, say nothing, and be nothing." And honestly, doing nothing sounds way worse than facing a little constructive feedback.

The Art of Taking Criticism Like a Pro

Over the years, I've developed a simple, three-step system for facing criticism without falling apart (or crying in the shower).

1. Pause Before Reacting

When someone criticizes you, your first instinct might be to get defensive or shut down. Trust me, I've been there. Like the time my boss told me my presentation had "room for improvement," and I immediately said, "Well, maybe your instructions had room for clarity!" (Spoiler: this did not go well.)

Take a breath. Count to five. Ask yourself, "Is this about me as a person, or just my work?" Most of the time, it's not personal—it's about the situation.

2. Look for the Truth (Even If It Hurts)

Not all criticism is created equal. Some of it is useful, and some of it is just noise. The trick is to separate the two.

- If your best friend says, "You're a little late sometimes," maybe it's worth setting an alarm five minutes earlier.
- If your aunt says, "You'll never make it as a writer," consider that she still thinks Facebook is "the email." Not all opinions deserve equal weight.

The truth is, even harsh criticism often has a nugget of wisdom. Extract it, and let the rest go.

3. Use Criticism as Fuel, Not Fire

Here's the secret: criticism is like manure. It stinks, but it helps things grow. The more you use it to improve, the less power it has to hurt you.

One time, I submitted an article to a publication I admired, and they rejected it with feedback so brutal I considered switching careers. But instead of quitting, I rewrote the article, applied their advice, and resubmitted it. Guess what? They accepted it the second time.

Critics don't get to decide your story. You do.

When Criticism Gets Personal

Not all criticism is constructive. Some people criticize out of jealousy, insecurity, or just because they're having a bad day. My personal low point came during my divorce, when someone said, "Well, I guess you weren't that great of a spouse, huh?"

Ouch.

In moments like these, remember this: their criticism says more about them than it does about you. As Eleanor Roosevelt put it, "No one can make you feel inferior without your consent."

A Funny Thing About Criticism

The funny thing about criticism is that it can teach you humility and resilience—two qualities that are surprisingly useful in life. For example, when my grandma used to tell me, "Honey, you look tired," I realized she wasn't being mean; she was just pointing out that I needed to slow down.

Even harsh criticism can be a gift in disguise. Like when my colleague once said, "You're great at starting things, but you don't always finish them." At first, I was offended. Then I realized he was right. That one comment helped me finish this book you're holding right now.

How to Critique Yourself Kindly

Let's flip the script for a moment. Sometimes the harshest critic we face is the one in our own head. Learning to critique yourself constructively is just as important as handling criticism from others.

Instead of saying, "I'm terrible at this," try saying, "This didn't go as planned, but here's how I can improve."

The Heart of Criticism

Criticism, at its core, is a reminder that you're growing, learning, and putting yourself out there. Sure, it stings in the moment. But it also sharpens you, strengthens you, and pushes you toward the person you're meant to become.

One of my favorite quotes is from Winston Churchill:

"To each, criticism is like pain in the body. It calls attention to an unhealthy state of things."

It's not about the pain—it's about what you do with it.

My Takeaway

As I write this chapter, I can't help but laugh at all the times criticism has humbled me. From that disastrous talent show performance to the feedback that reshaped my career, criticism has been both my greatest challenge and my greatest teacher.

So, the next time someone critiques you, take a deep breath. Thank them for their honesty (even if it's hard). And remember: every bit of feedback—whether it's a gentle nudge or a sharp jab—is an opportunity to grow.

And if all else fails, do what I do: pour yourself a cup of coffee, mutter "That's their opinion," and get back to work.

Chapter 7:
The Grit to Persist

How resilience is built in the face of repeated failure

Failure is inevitable. It is the great equalizer of ambition, testing not just our plans but also the depths of our resolve. Those who succeed in any field are not strangers to failure; rather, they are shaped by it. This chapter explores how resilience is cultivated through repeated setbacks and examines the mental, emotional, and practical tools that enable people to persist when the path forward seems insurmountable.

The Nature of Grit

Angela Duckworth, a prominent psychologist, defines grit as a combination of passion and perseverance directed toward long-term goals. While passion fuels the desire to achieve, perseverance keeps us moving forward despite obstacles. Grit is more than just a personality trait—it is a skill that can be honed through experience and reflection.

Resilience, a core component of grit, is forged in the crucible of failure. Each stumble, each rejection, and each misstep has the potential to either erode our confidence or strengthen our resolve. What determines the outcome is not the failure itself but how we respond to it.

Failure as a Teacher

When Thomas Edison famously stated, "I have not failed. I've just found 10,000 ways that won't work," he reframed failure as part of the learning process. This mindset—the ability to view setbacks as opportunities for growth—is central to building resilience.

Repeated failure forces us to confront uncomfortable truths about our limitations, strategies, or preparation. However, it also offers invaluable lessons. Each setback reveals something about our approach: Was our strategy flawed? Did we underestimate the challenge? Or were external factors beyond our control? By dissecting failure, we uncover the insights necessary to improve and try again.

Case in point: J.K. Rowling was rejected by multiple publishers before Harry Potter became a global phenomenon. Each rejection could have been the end of her journey. Instead, she refined her manuscript and persevered, ultimately building one of the most successful literary franchises in history.

The Psychology of Resilience

What happens in our minds when we fail? Neuroscience provides some answers. The brain's reward system releases dopamine when we succeed, reinforcing positive behavior. Conversely, failure can trigger the brain's stress response, leading to feelings of frustration or self-doubt.

However, the brain is remarkably adaptable. Studies show that individuals who view failure as a challenge rather than a threat are more likely to develop resilience. This mindset shift activates problem-solving areas of the brain, fostering creativity and determination.

Building Resilience

Resilience does not develop overnight. It is cultivated through deliberate effort and practice. The following strategies are instrumental in building the grit to persist:

1. Reframe Setbacks

Instead of viewing failure as evidence of inadequacy, treat it as feedback. What went wrong? What can you learn? The ability to pivot from despair to curiosity transforms failure into a stepping stone.

2. Set Incremental Goals

Breaking down long-term objectives into smaller, manageable tasks reduces the overwhelm of setbacks. Each small success reinforces the belief that progress is possible.

3. Cultivate a Growth Mindset

Coined by Carol Dweck, a growth mindset is the belief that abilities can be developed through effort and learning. This perspective fosters resilience by emphasizing improvement over innate talent.

4. Lean on Support Systems

No one succeeds in isolation. Friends, mentors, and peers provide encouragement, perspective, and sometimes the push needed to keep going.

5. Practice Self-Compassion

Being kind to yourself in moments of failure is not indulgent—it is essential. Harsh self-criticism can demoralize, while self-compassion creates space for recovery and reflection.

Stories of Grit

Throughout history, remarkable achievements have been the result of perseverance in the face of repeated failure:

- Walt Disney, who was fired for "lacking creativity," went on to revolutionize entertainment. His failures were stepping stones that refined his vision.
- Serena Williams, after injuries and personal setbacks, returned to dominate tennis because of her unwavering commitment to her craft.
- Nelson Mandela, who endured 27 years of imprisonment, emerged not broken but determined to dismantle apartheid, demonstrating unparalleled resilience.

These figures exemplify that failure is not the opposite of success; it is part of the journey.

The Role of Purpose

Grit thrives when it is anchored to a deep sense of purpose. Purpose gives meaning to the struggle and sustains motivation during the darkest moments. Viktor Frankl, a Holocaust survivor and psychologist, wrote in Man's Search for Meaning that those who found purpose in their suffering were more likely to endure and overcome.

For individuals pursuing ambitious goals, clarifying their "why" is essential. Why does this goal matter? Who will benefit from your success? Purpose transforms obstacles into challenges worth facing.

The Ripple Effect of Persistence

The resilience we build in the face of failure extends beyond individual achievement. It inspires others, creating a ripple effect. When we persist, we demonstrate that challenges can be overcome, encouraging others to confront their own fears of failure.

In organizations, leaders who model resilience create a culture where innovation and calculated risk-taking thrive. Teams become more adaptable, viewing setbacks as opportunities to pivot rather than reasons to quit.

Conclusion: Resilience Is a Muscle

Resilience is not a fixed trait; it is a muscle that grows stronger with use. Each failure provides an opportunity to exercise that muscle, pushing us closer to our goals. Grit, at its core, is the commitment to rise again, no matter how many times we fall.

The path to success is rarely a straight line. It twists and turns, demanding persistence, adaptability, and courage. But for those who embrace the process, failure becomes less a foe and more a mentor. To persist is to choose growth over comfort, and in that choice lies the foundation of resilience—and, ultimately, success.

Chapter 8:
From Regret to Redemption

Letting go of the past to focus on future growth

"Though no one can go back and make a brand-new start, anyone can start from now and make a brand-new ending."

—Carl Bard

Regret is a shadow that lingers, casting doubt over our choices and weighing heavily on our minds. It is a universal emotion, born from missed opportunities, wrong decisions, and paths untaken. Yet, regret is not a life sentence. While it may define a moment, it does not have to define our future. This chapter explores how to confront regret, learn from it, and transform it into a source of redemption and growth.

The Weight of Regret

"Regret for the things we did can be tempered by time; it is regret for the things we did not do that is inconsolable."

—Sydney J. Harris

Regret thrives in the silence of hindsight, magnifying our errors and creating a distorted narrative of failure. We dwell on what could have been and replay scenarios in our minds, wishing for different outcomes. These thoughts can become chains, binding us to the past and preventing us from embracing the present or moving toward the future.

Consider the story of Mary, a young woman who dreamed of becoming a painter. Fearing financial instability, she chose a practical career in accounting. Years later, she regretted shelving her passion, convinced she had missed her chance to create a meaningful life. For years, Mary's regret paralyzed her, until one day she decided to enroll in a local art class. That single step transformed her regret into a path toward redemption.

Why We Struggle to Let Go

"We are products of our past, but we don't have to be prisoners of it."

—Rick Warren

Letting go of regret is difficult because it is tied to deeply personal experiences—our dreams, relationships, and values. Often, we conflate our mistakes with our identity, believing that past failures define who we are. This self-criticism perpetuates a cycle of shame and inertia.

Psychologists refer to this as rumination: the tendency to obsessively think about negative events. While reflection can lead to insight, excessive rumination traps us in a loop, where regret becomes all-consuming. The key to breaking free lies in reframing how we view our past and ourselves.

The Bridge from Regret to Redemption

"When we deny our stories, they define us. When we own our stories, we can write a brave new ending."

—Brené Brown

Redemption begins with acknowledgment. To move forward, we must confront regret head-on and recognize it for what it is: an emotional response to unmet expectations or unfulfilled desires.

This acknowledgment allows us to process our feelings and identify the lessons hidden within our mistakes.

1. Forgive Yourself

"Forgive yourself for not knowing what you didn't know before you learned it."

—Maya Angelou

Self-forgiveness is the cornerstone of redemption. It involves accepting our imperfections and showing ourselves the same compassion we would extend to a friend. Without forgiveness, regret hardens into self-condemnation, stifling growth.

2. Extract the Lesson

"Failure is simply the opportunity to begin again, this time more intelligently."

—Henry Ford

Every regret carries a lesson. Whether it's a better understanding of our values, improved decision-making skills, or a reminder of what truly matters, these lessons shape us. Redemption comes when we use our regrets as stepping stones to wisdom.

3. Take Action in the Present

"Do what you can, with what you have, where you are."

—Theodore Roosevelt

Regret often paralyzes us by focusing our attention on what cannot be changed. The antidote is action. Small, deliberate steps in the present create momentum and shift our focus from what we lack to what we can build.

The Role of Redemption

"Redemption is not perfection. The redeemed must realize their imperfections."

—John Piper

Redemption is not about erasing the past but transforming it. It is the act of reclaiming agency over your life and rewriting your narrative. The most powerful stories of redemption are those in which individuals rise from their lowest points, not despite their regrets but because of them.

Consider Nelson Mandela, who spent 27 years in prison for his fight against apartheid. Instead of allowing bitterness to consume him, Mandela used his time in prison to reflect and prepare for a future of reconciliation. His journey from regret to redemption not only reshaped his life but also changed the course of history.

Practical Steps to Let Go

1. Reframe Regret

"Regret doesn't remind us that we did badly. It reminds us that we know we can do better."

—Kathryn Schulz

Reframing regret as evidence of your growth potential allows you to see it as a sign of your evolving values rather than a marker of failure.

2. Practice Gratitude

"Be thankful for what you have; you'll end up having more. If you concentrate on what you don't have, you will never, ever have enough."

—Oprah Winfrey

Gratitude shifts your focus from what you've lost to what you've gained. By appreciating the present, you weaken regret's grip on your mind.

3. Seek Closure

Sometimes, regret lingers because of unresolved conflicts or unmet goals. Writing a letter (even one you don't send), having a conversation, or creating a ritual to symbolize letting go can bring closure and peace.

4. Focus on the Future

"The best way to predict your future is to create it."

—Abraham Lincoln

Redemption is forward-focused. By setting new goals and committing to growth, you shift your energy from the past to the possibilities ahead.

Stories of Redemption

"Our greatest glory is not in never falling, but in rising every time we fall."

—Confucius

The annals of history are filled with stories of redemption. Malala Yousafzai turned a near-fatal attack into a platform for advocating girls' education worldwide. Oprah Winfrey overcame a traumatic childhood to become one of the most influential figures in media. These individuals are proof that regret can be a powerful catalyst for transformation.

Conclusion: The Freedom of Letting Go

"To err is human; to forgive, divine."

—Alexander Pope

Letting go of regret is an act of liberation. It frees us from the chains of the past and empowers us to shape our destiny. Redemption does not mean forgetting or erasing; it means carrying forward the lessons and leaving behind the weight.

The road from regret to redemption is not linear. It requires courage, patience, and a willingness to face the truth. But for those who persist, the reward is profound: a life unburdened by what was, and rich with the potential of what could be.

Chapter 9:
Losing Them

"Grief never truly leaves you. It just teaches you how to carry it."

My grandparents were my world. They were my foundation, my safe haven, the two people who saw the best in me even when I couldn't see it in myself. Losing them wasn't just a blow—it was a collapse.

I remember the day I lost my grandmother as clearly as if it happened yesterday. Her laugh, her cooking, her way of making everyone feel seen—it was like God's love wrapped in human form. And when she left, it felt like the air in the room left with her.

Grief has a strange way of creeping up on you. One moment, you're laughing at a memory, and the next, you're in tears because you realize you'll never make another one.

The Weight of Loss

When I lost my grandmother, it was like the last light in my world went out. They were gone. Both of them. And no matter how much I prayed or begged, they weren't coming back.

I tried to find comfort in the fact that they were with God, but it felt hollow. I wanted them here. I wanted one more hug, one more conversation, one more moment to say, *Thank you for loving me when I didn't even love myself.*

But grief doesn't give you those moments. It just leaves you with the emptiness of what could've been.

A Lesson in Legacy

In my pain, I found myself returning to the lessons they had taught me. My grandfather always said, *"When life gets hard, don't run from it—run through it. That's where your strength is."* My grandmother used to remind me, *"The Lord giveth, and the Lord taketh away. But baby, He never leaves you empty-handed."*

I didn't understand those words at first. I thought God had left me with nothing. But as I sat in their absence, I realized they had left me something priceless: a legacy of faith.

"Blessed Are Those Who Mourn"

Jesus said in Matthew 5:4, *"Blessed are those who mourn, for they will be comforted."* I clung to that verse, even when comfort felt far away. I realized that mourning isn't a sign of weakness—it's a testament to love.

You don't grieve what you don't value. And my grief for them was a reflection of how deeply they had impacted my life.

Finding Them in the Small Things

Over time, I began to find my grandparents in the little things. I heard my grandfather's voice in the stillness of my struggles, reminding me to keep going. I felt my grandmother's presence in the kindness of strangers, the smell of cornbread baking, and the songs I sang in church.

They were gone, but they were never truly gone. They had become a part of me.

Grief as a Teacher

Grief taught me that love doesn't end with death. It transforms. It becomes the memories you carry, the lessons you pass on, and the strength you didn't know you had.

Losing them broke me, but it also built me. It reminded me that life is fleeting, but love is eternal. And as long as I live, I'll carry their love with me, letting it guide me through the darkest of days.

Chapter 10:
Iterative Improvement

The power of incremental change and small wins after setbacks

"Do not despise these small beginnings, for the Lord rejoices to see the work begin."

—Zechariah 4:10

In life, it's easy to dream big but feel paralyzed by the weight of those dreams. When faced with setbacks, the gap between where we are and where we want to be can seem insurmountable. Yet, progress doesn't demand perfection—it demands persistence. Incremental improvement, the practice of making small but consistent changes, is the most reliable path to transformation.

This chapter is a rallying cry for those who feel discouraged by failure. It's a reminder that progress, no matter how small, is still progress. Small wins after setbacks are like stepping stones across a river: individually, they may seem insignificant, but together, they carry you to the other side.

The Power of Small Steps

"Success is the sum of small efforts, repeated day in and day out."

—Robert Collier

When you're rebuilding after a setback, grand gestures and sweeping changes can feel overwhelming. That's why the concept of iterative improvement—breaking a large goal into manageable steps—is so effective.

Imagine a sculptor chiseling a block of marble. They don't reveal a masterpiece with a single swing of the hammer. Instead, each small, deliberate strike removes unnecessary material and brings the vision closer to life. The same principle applies to personal growth, professional goals, and overcoming adversity.

Consider Thomas Edison's journey to invent the electric light bulb. It took over 1,000 failed attempts before he succeeded. Rather than focusing on failure, Edison saw each attempt as a step forward, famously stating, "I have not failed. I've just found 10,000 ways that won't work." His story demonstrates that the cumulative power of small, iterative improvements can create revolutionary results.

Why Incremental Change Works

1. Momentum Builds Confidence

"A journey of a thousand miles begins with a single step."

—Lao Tzu

Each small win acts as fuel for the next. When you achieve a minor goal, your brain releases dopamine, a chemical associated with motivation and happiness. This creates a feedback loop: success breeds confidence, which drives more success.

2. Mistakes Become Manageable

When you focus on small changes, the stakes are lower. A mistake in one small area doesn't derail the entire process—it becomes an opportunity to course-correct without overwhelming consequences.

3. Sustainable Growth

Big changes often demand significant resources—time, energy, and willpower. Small, incremental changes, however, are easier to sustain over time. This makes the process of improvement feel less like a sprint and more like a marathon.

From Setback to Small Wins

"The steps of a good man are ordered by the Lord, and He delights in his way. Though he fall, he shall not be utterly cast down; for the Lord upholds him with His hand."

—Psalm 37:23-24

After a setback, the temptation is to either rush toward a massive comeback or give up entirely. But there's a better way: focus on one small step. Small wins may seem trivial at first, but they restore a sense of control and lay the foundation for greater victories.

Case Study: The "1% Rule" in Sports

Dave Brailsford, coach of the British Cycling team, implemented a strategy of marginal gains—improving every aspect of performance by just 1%. He and his team analyzed everything: the design of the bike, the diet of the riders, even the best pillows for sleep. The result? A decade of dominance, including multiple Tour de France wins and Olympic gold medals.

The takeaway is clear: incremental improvements compound over time, leading to extraordinary outcomes.

Strategies for Iterative Improvement

1. Start Small and Build

"Whoever can be trusted with very little can also be trusted with much."

—Luke 16:10

Pick one area where you can make progress today. It could be as simple as organizing your workspace, setting aside 10 minutes to exercise, or reaching out to a mentor. Small wins create momentum.

2. Track Your Progress

"Write the vision; make it plain on tablets, so he may run who reads it."

—Habakkuk 2:2

Progress is easier to recognize when it's documented. Keep a journal or use an app to track your goals. Seeing your journey laid out in front of you is incredibly motivating.

3. Focus on the Process, Not Perfection

"Let us not become weary in doing good, for at the proper time we will reap a harvest if we do not give up."

—Galatians 6:9

Success isn't about flawless execution—it's about consistent effort. Focus on improving 1% every day rather than trying to leap to 100% overnight.

4. Celebrate Every Victory

"Rejoice in the Lord always; again I will say, rejoice."

—Philippians 4:4

No win is too small to celebrate. Recognizing your achievements, no matter how minor, reinforces positive behavior and keeps you motivated.

5. Adapt and Adjust

"In their hearts humans plan their course, but the Lord establishes their steps."

—Proverbs 16:9

Life is unpredictable, and setbacks are inevitable. Embrace flexibility. If one strategy doesn't work, adapt your approach without losing sight of your goal.

The Compound Effect of Small Wins

"So let's not get tired of doing what is good. At just the right time we will reap a harvest of blessing if we don't give up."

—Galatians 6:9

Small, consistent changes lead to exponential growth. This principle, known as the compound effect, demonstrates that even tiny actions, repeated consistently, yield remarkable results over time.

For instance, saving just $5 a day may seem insignificant. Yet, over a year, that's $1,825. With compound interest, it grows into much more. The same principle applies to personal growth: reading one page a day leads to finishing multiple books in a year. Writing one paragraph daily results in a completed manuscript.

Real-Life Redemption Through Small Wins

"And let us run with perseverance the race marked out for us, fixing our eyes on Jesus, the pioneer and perfecter of faith."

—Hebrews 12:1-2

Consider Sarah, a single mother who lost her job and felt overwhelmed by the weight of her responsibilities. Instead of trying to fix everything at once, she focused on small steps: updating her resume, applying to one job per day, and taking free online courses to improve her skills. Each step brought her closer to stability. A year later, Sarah secured a better-paying job, started a side business, and felt stronger than ever.

Her story illustrates how small, consistent actions can rebuild confidence, create opportunity, and restore hope.

Conclusion: Keep Climbing

"The path of the righteous is like the morning sun, shining ever brighter till the full light of day."

—Proverbs 4:18

Iterative improvement is a commitment to growth, one step at a time. It's about recognizing that even the smallest progress moves you closer to your goals. When you string together enough small wins, you create momentum that is unstoppable.

You don't need to leap to the finish line today. Take one step. Then another. Trust the process and celebrate each victory, no matter how small. Remember, the power of incremental change is not just in where it takes you—it's in who you become along the way.

So keep going. Start small, aim high, and never stop climbing.

Chapter 11:
Married Too Soon

"Love is beautiful, but it isn't always enough."

I was 19 when I got married. Too young to know the weight of forever but old enough to believe in it. We were kids trying to play house, thinking love alone could build a home.

At first, it felt like a dream. We had laughter, passion, and promises whispered in the dark. But love, as I would later learn, needs more than feelings to survive. It needs growth, understanding, and maturity—things we didn't have yet.

The Cracks in the Foundation

We started with so much hope, but over time, the cracks began to show. Arguments about money, unmet expectations, and the silent resentment that comes when two people drift apart.

I wanted to be her rock, her provider, her everything. But how could I be that when I didn't even know who I was?

The Slow Unraveling

There's a moment in every failing marriage when you realize it's slipping away. For me, it was the night we sat at opposite ends of the couch, saying nothing. The silence was louder than any argument we'd ever had.

I remember looking at her and thinking, *We're here, but we're not really here.* We had become strangers in the same house.

Lessons in Love

The divorce at 28 was like a death. I grieved the life we could've had, the dreams we had built together. But in that grief, I also learned something important: love is a gift, but it's not always forever.

And that's okay. Some people come into your life to teach you, to shape you, and to help you grow. She wasn't my forever, but she was my lesson.

Finding Peace in the Pain

One night, I prayed, "God, why didn't it work? Why did You let us fail?" And I felt Him answer, *"Because you weren't ready. And that's okay."*

I learned that failure in love doesn't mean failure as a person. It means you're still learning. And one day, when the time is right, love will come again—stronger, deeper, and wiser.

Chapter: A New Kind of Hope

"Hope isn't just wishful thinking—it's a declaration that tomorrow can be better, even when today feels impossible."

Hope is a fragile thing, especially when life has beaten you down. It's easy to lose sight of it when your circumstances scream failure, rejection, and despair. But I learned that hope isn't about what you see—it's about what you believe.

And belief, as I discovered, is a choice.

The Weight of the Past

Even as I began to rebuild my life, the weight of my past threatened to drag me down. There were moments when I couldn't look in the mirror without seeing my failures staring back at me.

The enemy loves to remind you of what you've lost, of where you've been. He whispers, *You're not good enough. You'll never make it.*

But then I'd remember Lamentations 3:22-23:

"Because of the Lord's great love, we are not consumed, for His compassions never fail. They are new every morning; great is Your faithfulness."

That verse became my lifeline. Every morning, I told myself: *Today is a new day. His mercies are new. I don't have to be defined by yesterday.*

Small Steps Forward

Hope doesn't come all at once. It comes in small, quiet steps.

For me, it started with the simple act of getting up each day and choosing to believe that God still had a plan for me. I found a job, saved what little I could, and slowly started to rebuild.

There were setbacks, of course. Times when I felt like giving up. But every time I stumbled, God reminded me, *You're not walking this road alone.*

A Community of Believers

One of the greatest gifts God gave me during this time was a community of people who believed in me when I couldn't believe in myself.

My parents, Siblings and aunts and uncles didn't care about my past—they cared about my future. They encouraged me, prayed with me, and reminded me that I was still worthy of love and purpose.

Their kindness gave me hope. It showed me that God often works through people to bring His light into our darkest moments.

The Power of Giving Back

As I began to heal, I realized that hope isn't something you keep to yourself—it's something you give away.

I started volunteering at shelters, sharing my story with people who were where I had been. I told them, "I know it's hard. I know it feels impossible. But I'm standing here as proof that God can bring beauty from ashes."

Helping others gave me a new sense of purpose. It reminded me that even in my brokenness, I could still make a difference.

Hope in Action

One day, a young man approached me after I spoke at a community center. He was homeless, jobless, and ready to give up. "How did you do it?" he asked. "How did you keep going?"

I looked him in the eyes and said, "I didn't. God did. I just trusted Him to carry me when I couldn't carry myself."

I shared with him one of my favorite quotes:

"When you reach the end of your rope, tie a knot and hang on."
– Franklin D. Roosevelt

He nodded, tears in his eyes. "I think I can do that," he said.

And that's the thing about hope—it's contagious.

A New Perspective

Hope doesn't mean life will suddenly be easy. It doesn't mean you'll never face challenges again. But it does mean you can face them with the assurance that God is with you, that better days are ahead, and that you are stronger than you think.

Romans 5:3-5 says, *"We also glory in our sufferings, because we know that suffering produces perseverance; perseverance, character; and character, hope. And hope does not put us to shame, because God's love has been poured out into our hearts."*

That verse became my anthem. It reminded me that every trial I faced had a purpose, and that purpose was to build something unshakable within me.

Living with Hope

Hope became my fuel. It gave me the strength to keep moving forward, to dream again, to believe that my story wasn't over.

And as I stood on the other side of rock bottom, I realized something profound:

Hope isn't about avoiding the storms—it's about knowing the sun will shine again.

Chapter 12:
The Role of Mentors and Allies

How others can help you navigate through failure and emerge stronger

"If you want to go fast, go alone. If you want to go far, go together."

—African Proverb

No one succeeds alone. Behind every triumph lies a network of mentors, allies, and supporters who guide, challenge, and uplift. When failure strikes, these people become even more vital—not as saviors but as partners in your growth. They offer wisdom when you're lost, encouragement when you're discouraged, and accountability when you're tempted to give up.

This chapter explores the transformative power of mentors and allies. It's a reminder that even in your darkest moments, you don't have to walk the path alone.

The Power of Guidance

"Plans fail for lack of counsel, but with many advisers, they succeed."

—Proverbs 15:22

Mentors and allies serve as your compass during times of uncertainty. They provide perspective and insights you may not see on your own. A good mentor isn't there to solve your problems but to help you uncover solutions within yourself.

Consider the example of J.R.R. Tolkien mentoring C.S. Lewis. When Lewis doubted his abilities as a writer, Tolkien offered feedback, encouragement, and camaraderie. Their collaboration didn't just produce timeless works of literature—it helped Lewis overcome self-doubt and find his creative voice.

Why You Need Mentors and Allies

"A mentor doesn't light the path for you; they teach you how to find the light yourself."

—W.J. Simpson

1. They Offer Perspective

After failure, it's easy to get trapped in negative thinking. A mentor or ally can help you zoom out, seeing the bigger picture. They remind you that setbacks are temporary and growth is possible.

2. They Shorten the Learning Curve

Mentors have often walked the path you're on. Their experience can save you from unnecessary mistakes, accelerating your growth.

3. They Hold You Accountable

Allies provide the accountability needed to stay on track. They challenge you to act on your goals and follow through, even when motivation wanes.

4. They Celebrate Wins with You

Having someone in your corner to celebrate your progress, no matter how small, can reignite your passion and keep you moving forward.

How to Find the Right Mentors and Allies

"The right people don't just guide your steps—they remind you why you're walking the path in the first place."

—W.J. Simpson

Finding the right mentors and allies isn't about luck; it's about intentionality. Here's how to build your network of support:

1. Look for Shared Values

Seek people whose principles align with yours. A mentor who understands your purpose will offer guidance that resonates with your goals.

2. Diversify Your Network

Don't limit yourself to one mentor or ally. Surround yourself with a variety of voices—people who challenge you, inspire you, and bring unique perspectives to the table.

3. Be Willing to Ask

The best relationships often start with a simple question: "Can you help me?" People are often more willing to mentor or support you than you think.

4. Be a Good Mentee or Ally

Show gratitude, respect their time, and take action on their advice. Being a good mentee strengthens the relationship and makes them more invested in your growth.

Types of Mentors and Allies You Need

1. The Encourager

This person lifts you up when failure knocks you down. They remind you of your strengths and potential when you can't see it yourself.

2. The Challenger

The challenger doesn't sugarcoat things. They push you out of your comfort zone, asking the tough questions and holding you to high standards.

3. The Expert

With years of experience, the expert offers practical advice and insights, helping you avoid pitfalls and make informed decisions.

4. The Peer

Sometimes, the best support comes from someone who's walking the same path. Peers share experiences, empathy, and camaraderie, reminding you that you're not alone.

Biblical Examples of Mentorship and Allyship

The Bible is rich with stories of mentors and allies who helped others navigate failure and achieve greatness:

- Moses and Joshua: Moses mentored Joshua, preparing him to lead Israel into the Promised Land. Even after setbacks in the wilderness, Moses's guidance helped Joshua grow into a confident leader.
- Naomi and Ruth: After experiencing loss and failure, Naomi became a mentor to Ruth, guiding her toward a brighter future. Their bond was built on loyalty, love, and shared purpose.
- Paul and Timothy: Paul served as a spiritual mentor to Timothy, encouraging him to persevere in faith and leadership despite challenges.

These examples show the profound impact of mentorship and allyship in overcoming adversity.

Practical Steps to Build Your Support System

"Your circle determines your trajectory. Surround yourself with those who believe in your vision and challenge you to pursue it relentlessly."

—W.J. Simpson

1. Cultivate Relationships Intentionally

Invest time and energy into building meaningful connections. Attend events, join communities, or reach out to people you admire.

2. Give as Much as You Take

Mentorship and allyship are two-way streets. Offer your own insights, support, and encouragement in return.

3. Regularly Seek Feedback

Ask for constructive feedback from mentors and allies. Be open to their insights, even when it's uncomfortable.

4. Create a Safe Space for Growth

Surround yourself with people who foster growth, not negativity. Trust and mutual respect are the foundation of any strong relationship.

The Transformative Power of Allies

"Two are better than one, because they have a good return for their labor: If either of them falls down, one can help the other up."

—Ecclesiastes 4:9-10

Failure can feel isolating, but allies make the journey bearable. They remind you of your worth when you doubt yourself, and they offer strength when yours falters.

Consider the story of Thomas Edison, whose many failed attempts to invent the lightbulb were supported by a team of dedicated collaborators. Their collective efforts transformed failure into innovation.

The Ripple Effect of Mentorship

"Mentorship isn't just about guiding someone; it's about creating a ripple of growth that touches countless lives."

—W.J. Simpson

When you benefit from mentors and allies, you're not the only one who grows. By sharing your lessons and paying it forward, you become a mentor or ally for someone else. The cycle of support and growth continues, creating a ripple effect that extends far beyond you.

Conclusion: Together, We Rise

"The greatest strength is found not in solitude but in community."

—W.J. Simpson

In the face of failure, mentors and allies are your anchor, your compass, and your strength. They remind you that every setback is a setup for a comeback—and you don't have to face it alone.

Seek out mentors who inspire you and allies who uplift you. Lean on them, learn from them, and let their support propel you forward. And as you rise, don't forget to turn around and help someone else along the way.

Because the truth is, we rise higher when we rise together.

Chapter 13:
When Failure Leads to Innovation

Why some of the greatest breakthroughs come from mistakes

"Failure doesn't close the door to success; it opens a window you never knew existed."

—W.J. Simpson

There's a peculiar magic in failure. It stings, frustrates, and humbles—but it also pushes boundaries. Often, failure isn't the end of the story; it's the twist that leads to something greater. Some of history's greatest breakthroughs were born from unintended outcomes. This chapter explores how failure, when embraced and analyzed, can become the catalyst for groundbreaking innovation.

To illustrate this, we'll journey through a fictional story of invention—a tale that embodies how setbacks can spark creativity and lead to extraordinary success.

The Tale of Elena and the Invisible Thread

The Big Dream

Elena Vasquez was a young materials scientist with a dream of revolutionizing wearable technology. Fresh out of university, she joined a start-up focused on creating ultra-thin, flexible fabrics that could conduct electricity. Her team envisioned smart clothing that could monitor health metrics, charge devices, and even interact with augmented reality systems.

Elena's role was to develop the conductive thread—the backbone of their vision. It needed to be durable, affordable, and capable of seamlessly integrating into fabric. Months of research led her to a promising alloy, but early tests were disappointing. The threads were too brittle, snapping under minimal pressure.

Despite the setbacks, Elena refused to give up. She worked long nights in the lab, tweaking the alloy's composition and experimenting with different manufacturing techniques.

The Breaking Point

One evening, after yet another failed test, Elena felt crushed. She sat in the dimly lit lab, staring at a pile of broken threads. The deadline for their prototype presentation was weeks away, and her team was depending on her.

"Why can't I get this right?" she muttered, gripping her head in frustration.

As she absentmindedly adjusted the settings on the lab's laser cutter, she noticed a strange shimmer on the table. One of the failed threads had split open, revealing an intricate, web-like pattern. It wasn't what she had been aiming for, but something about it caught her attention.

Curious, she tested the thread's conductivity. To her astonishment, the split structure enhanced its performance, allowing it to carry more electricity without overheating. She ran more tests and discovered that the "failure" wasn't a flaw—it was an opportunity.

Turning Failure Into Innovation

The brittle alloy had inadvertently created a self-healing mechanism: when the thread broke, it restructured itself into a stronger, more conductive form. Elena realized that instead of fighting the material's properties, she could work with them.

She pitched the idea to her team: what if they pivoted their focus from traditional wearable tech to adaptive materials that could repair themselves? The team was skeptical but intrigued. They decided to take the risk.

After months of refinement, Elena's self-healing threads became the centerpiece of a groundbreaking product line. The technology attracted investors, and their start-up secured a multimillion-dollar contract with a major tech company. What began as a failure had transformed into a revolutionary innovation.

Why Failure Fuels Innovation

"Failure strips away assumptions and forces us to see problems from new angles."

—W.J. Simpson

Elena's story reflects a fundamental truth: failure often reveals paths we never considered. Here's why failure can lead to innovation:

1. Failure Forces Rethinking

When something doesn't work, it pushes us to question our assumptions and explore alternatives. The rigidity of our plans softens, allowing creativity to flow.

2. Failure Reveals Hidden Opportunities

Many breakthroughs come from unintended results. From penicillin to the microwave oven, history is filled with examples of accidental discoveries born from failure.

3. Failure Builds Resilience

The process of overcoming failure strengthens problem-solving skills and perseverance—essential traits for innovation.

Real-World Examples of Failure Leading to Breakthroughs

1. Post-it Notes

In the 1960s, Spencer Silver, a scientist at 3M, was trying to create a super-strong adhesive. Instead, he developed a weak, pressure-sensitive glue that didn't seem useful. Years later, a colleague used the adhesive to create sticky bookmarks—and the Post-it Note was born.

2. The Creation of Velcro

Swiss engineer George de Mestral noticed how burrs clung to his dog's fur after a walk in the woods. Inspired by this "annoyance," he invented Velcro, which became a ubiquitous fastening material.

3. Penicillin

Alexander Fleming's accidental discovery of penicillin came when mold contaminated his petri dishes. What looked like a ruined experiment became the foundation for modern antibiotics.

Embracing Failure as a Tool for Innovation

"The key to innovation isn't avoiding failure; it's learning to embrace it."

—W.J. Simpson

Here's how you can harness failure for innovation in your own life:

1. Shift Your Perspective

Instead of seeing failure as the end, view it as part of the process. Ask yourself: What is this teaching me?

2. Experiment Fearlessly

Innovation thrives on experimentation. Be willing to test ideas, knowing some will fail. Each attempt brings you closer to success.

3. Collaborate with Others

Elena's breakthrough came from involving her team in her pivot. Surround yourself with people who can help you see possibilities in failure.

4. Stay Curious

Curiosity turns setbacks into opportunities. Look for patterns, anomalies, and unexpected outcomes that might lead to something new.

Biblical Insights on Failure and Innovation

The Bible often shows how failure can lead to greater purpose:

- Joseph's Journey: Sold into slavery and imprisoned, Joseph's apparent failures set the stage for him to rise as a leader in Egypt, ultimately saving his family during a famine (Genesis 50:20).
- The Apostle Paul: Before becoming a missionary, Paul faced failure in his early ministry attempts. Yet, these experiences shaped him into one of Christianity's greatest evangelists.
- Peter's Denial: Peter's failure in denying Jesus three times could have defined him. Instead, it became the turning point for his bold leadership in spreading the gospel.

These stories remind us that failure isn't the end—it's often the beginning of something greater.

Conclusion: The Gift of Failure

"Failure doesn't just break barriers; it builds bridges to possibilities we never imagined."

—W.J. Simpson

Elena's story, like so many real-life breakthroughs, shows us that failure isn't something to fear—it's something to embrace. It forces us to think differently, challenges our assumptions, and sparks innovation in ways success never could.

The next time you face a setback, ask yourself: What's the hidden opportunity here? You might be surprised by what you discover.

Remember, every failure carries within it the seeds of innovation. All you have to do is look closely, stay curious, and keep moving forward.

Chapter 14:
Failing as a Leader

Navigating missteps in leadership and inspiring others through vulnerability

"Leadership is not about being perfect; it's about being courageous enough to admit your flaws, learn from them, and guide others to do the same."

—W.J. Simpson

Leadership is both a privilege and a responsibility, and it comes with an expectation of vision, decisiveness, and strength. However, even the most experienced leaders stumble. Mistakes are inevitable because leadership involves making decisions in uncertain, high-pressure situations. The key isn't avoiding failure but responding to it in a way that builds trust, fosters growth, and inspires others.

This chapter delves into the reality of leadership failure, showing how vulnerability and resilience can turn a misstep into a defining moment. Whether you're a pastor, a city official, or a politician, failure as a leader is not the end—it can be the foundation of deeper, more authentic leadership.

The Burden of Leadership Failure

Leadership failure carries a unique weight. When leaders falter, the impact ripples across teams, organizations, and communities. For a pastor, a misstep might challenge the faith of a congregation. For a city official, an oversight might disrupt the lives of constituents. For a politician, an error might erode public trust.

This responsibility amplifies the pain of failure, but it also holds immense potential for growth. People look to leaders not for perfection, but for honesty, accountability, and the ability to rise again.

A Story of Redemption: Mayor Jameson's Misstep

The Mistake

Mayor Rachel Jameson was beloved by her city. She was a visionary leader, known for her community-first approach. But in her second term, she made a critical error. In an effort to fast-track a major urban development project, she approved it without fully vetting the environmental impact.

Within months, flooding in the affected area displaced dozens of families, and the media was relentless in its coverage. Protesters gathered outside city hall, and her approval ratings plummeted. For the first time in her career, Rachel felt like a failure.

The Turning Point

Instead of hiding from the backlash, Mayor Jameson did something unexpected: she stood before a packed city council meeting and publicly took responsibility.

"I made a mistake," she said, her voice steady but filled with emotion. "In my haste to bring progress, I overlooked the voices that warned me. To the families who have suffered, I am deeply sorry. I promise to make this right—not with words, but with action."

Her vulnerability surprised everyone. Critics softened, and her supporters rallied. She worked tirelessly to relocate affected families and launched a new task force to ensure all future projects prioritized environmental and community impact.

The Redemption

By the end of her term, Mayor Jameson's transparency and determination had restored trust. She was re-elected, not because she was perfect, but because she proved that even in failure, she was a leader worth following.

The Leadership Paradox: Strength in Vulnerability

"To admit failure is not to show weakness—it is to demonstrate the strength to grow beyond it."

—W.J. Simpson

True leadership isn't about projecting an image of invincibility. It's about embodying humanity, humility, and resilience. Here's why vulnerability in failure strengthens leadership:

1. It Builds Trust

Admitting mistakes shows integrity and authenticity. People are more likely to follow a leader who is honest about their shortcomings.

2. It Inspires Growth

A leader's willingness to learn from failure sets an example for others to do the same, creating a culture of continuous improvement.

3. It Deepens Connection

Vulnerability humanizes leaders, fostering empathy and loyalty among those they serve.

Biblical Lessons on Leadership and Failure

The Bible offers profound examples of leaders who failed but ultimately fulfilled their purpose through humility and reliance on God:

- King David: David's failure with Bathsheba and the consequences that followed could have destroyed his reign. Instead, his heartfelt repentance (Psalm 51) and renewed focus on God demonstrated his strength as a leader.
- Moses: Despite his anger leading to disobedience when striking the rock (Numbers 20:10-12), Moses remained a model of servant leadership, guiding Israel with humility and perseverance.
- Peter: After denying Jesus three times, Peter might have walked away from leadership altogether. Instead, he accepted grace, grew in faith, and became a cornerstone of the early church (John 21:15-19).

These stories remind us that failure doesn't disqualify a leader—it refines them.

Steps to Navigate Leadership Failure

1. Acknowledge the Mistake

"The first step toward rebuilding trust is taking responsibility."

When failure occurs, resist the urge to deflect blame. Acknowledging the mistake openly demonstrates accountability and respect for those you serve.

2. Seek Feedback

Engage with your team or community to understand the impact of your actions. This not only informs your next steps but also shows that you value their input.

3. Reflect and Learn

Failure is a teacher. Ask yourself: What led to this outcome? What could I have done differently? Use these insights to improve future decisions.

4. Take Corrective Action

Words must be followed by action. Develop and implement a plan to address the consequences of your mistake. This demonstrates commitment to growth and responsibility.

5. Model Resilience

Your response to failure sets the tone for those you lead. Show that setbacks are opportunities for growth, not reasons to give up.

Practical Advice for Leaders in All Spheres

1. Pastors: When sermons miss the mark or decisions cause division, acknowledge the misstep. Use it as an opportunity to model Christ-like humility and reconciliation.

2. City Officials: Engage directly with affected communities when policies fall short. Listening sessions and transparent communication can rebuild trust.

3. Politicians: Own up to mistakes publicly and present tangible solutions. Integrity and action resonate far more than defensiveness or denial.

Quotes to Reflect On

- "A leader's greatness is measured not by their achievements but by their ability to rise after failure." —Original
- "He who is greatest among you shall be your servant." —Matthew 23:11
- "The ultimate test of leadership is not avoiding mistakes but mastering the art of recovery." —Original

Conclusion: Leadership Through Failure

Leadership isn't a straight path to success—it's a winding journey marked by challenges, mistakes, and moments of self-doubt. Yet, the greatest leaders aren't defined by their failures; they're defined by how they respond to them.

As a leader, your vulnerability can inspire. Your resilience can motivate. And your humility can transform mistakes into milestones. Whether you're guiding a congregation, a city, or a nation, remember this: the world doesn't need perfect leaders. It needs leaders who rise stronger, wiser, and more compassionate after they fall.

Because in the end, leadership is not about avoiding failure—it's about embracing it as a stepping stone to greatness.

Chapter 15:
The Risk-Reward Equation

Understanding calculated risks and embracing uncertainty

"The greatest rewards often lie just beyond the edge of uncertainty."

—W.J. Simpson

Life is full of opportunities, but seizing them often requires risk. Whether starting a new business, launching a community initiative, or making a personal leap of faith, every worthwhile venture carries uncertainty. The fear of failure can paralyze, but understanding the risk-reward equation allows us to make informed decisions and embrace uncertainty as a necessary component of growth.

In this chapter, we explore how to evaluate risks, find the courage to act despite uncertainty, and reap the rewards of bold yet thoughtful decisions.

What Is the Risk-Reward Equation?

The risk-reward equation is simple in principle: the greater the risk, the greater the potential reward. However, the equation isn't about recklessness. It's about calculated risks—decisions made with careful consideration of the potential outcomes, both positive and negative.

Successful risk-takers aren't fearless; they are strategic. They assess their options, weigh the consequences, and then act decisively.

The goal is not to eliminate uncertainty but to manage it effectively.

A Story of Risk and Reward: The Bakery That Almost Wasn't

The Dream

Caleb Turner had always dreamed of opening his own bakery. For years, he worked as a pastry chef in someone else's kitchen, perfecting his craft and saving every spare dollar. Finally, an opportunity arose: a prime location in the heart of his city became available.

But there was a catch. The lease required a hefty upfront investment, and Caleb's savings wouldn't cover it. He would need to take out a substantial loan, putting not only his finances but also his family's stability on the line.

The Dilemma

Caleb wrestled with the decision. What if the bakery failed? What if he couldn't repay the loan? But as he listed the risks, he also considered the potential rewards: building a business that reflected his passion, creating jobs in his community, and leaving a legacy for his children.

He spent weeks researching, consulting with financial advisors, and surveying the neighborhood to gauge demand. Armed with data and a clear plan, Caleb decided to take the leap.

The Outcome

The first year was challenging. Caleb worked long hours, and there were moments he questioned his decision. But his calculated risk paid off. The bakery became a beloved neighborhood staple, celebrated for its creativity and quality. Five years later, Caleb opened a second location.

Had Caleb avoided the risk, he would have remained in the safety of someone else's kitchen—but he also would have missed the chance to build something truly his own.

The Anatomy of Calculated Risks

Taking a risk doesn't mean diving in blindly. It means following a process of thoughtful evaluation:

1. Define Your Goal

Clearly articulate what you hope to achieve. Is it personal growth, financial success, or societal impact? Knowing your "why" helps guide your decisions.

2. Assess the Risks

What could go wrong? Identify potential obstacles, challenges, and worst-case scenarios. This isn't about discouraging action but preparing for reality.

3. Evaluate the Rewards

What's the potential upside? Consider both tangible rewards (financial gain, career advancement) and intangible ones (fulfillment, personal growth).

4. Mitigate the Risks

How can you reduce uncertainty? This might involve gathering more information, creating a backup plan, or seeking guidance from mentors.

5. Make the Decision

At some point, you have to move from analysis to action. Accept that no decision is risk-free and trust the process you've followed.

The Role of Faith in Risk-Taking

Faith plays a significant role in navigating the unknown. For many, faith provides the courage to step forward even when the path isn't clear. The Bible is filled with stories of individuals who embraced uncertainty and were rewarded for their trust in God.

- Abraham: God called Abraham to leave his home and journey to an unknown land (Genesis 12:1-4). Abraham took the risk, trusting God's promise, and became the father of nations.
- Esther: Queen Esther risked her life to approach the king and save her people (Esther 4:14-16). Her courage in the face of uncertainty changed the course of history.
- The Parable of the Talents: Jesus praised the servant who took a risk by investing his talents, while the one who buried his out of fear was reprimanded (Matthew 25:14-30).

Faith doesn't eliminate risk but provides the strength to face it with confidence.

The Intersection of Leadership and Risk

For leaders, the ability to take calculated risks is essential. Whether you're a pastor introducing a new ministry, a city official pursuing a controversial policy, or a CEO launching a new product, your decisions impact others.

- Transparency: Communicate the reasons behind your decision. This builds trust and helps others understand the potential rewards and risks.
- Collaboration: Involve others in the decision-making process. Diverse perspectives can uncover blind spots and improve outcomes.
- Resilience: Be prepared to adapt if things don't go as planned. True leaders use setbacks as stepping stones to greater achievements.

Real-Life Examples of Bold Risks

- Martin Luther King Jr.: Leading the civil rights movement was an extraordinary risk. Dr. King faced imprisonment, threats, and ultimately death. Yet, his courage inspired a nation and brought about lasting change.
- Elon Musk: Musk bet his personal fortune on companies like Tesla and SpaceX, risking bankruptcy to pursue his vision. Today, those risks have redefined industries.
- Rosa Parks: By refusing to give up her bus seat, Rosa Parks risked her safety but ignited a movement that transformed America's social fabric.

Overcoming the Fear of Failure

"Fear asks, 'What if I fail?' Courage asks, 'What if I don't try?'"

—W.J. Simpson

Fear of failure is the greatest barrier to taking risks. Here's how to overcome it:

1. Focus on Growth: View risks as opportunities to learn and grow, regardless of the outcome.

2. Start Small: Take smaller risks to build confidence for bigger decisions.

3. Seek Support: Surround yourself with people who encourage and challenge you.

4. Reframe Failure: Remember, failure isn't the opposite of success; it's part of the journey.

Quotes to Remember

- "Fortune favors the brave." —Latin Proverb
- "Faith is taking the first step even when you don't see the whole staircase." —Martin Luther King Jr.
- "In their hearts, humans plan their course, but the Lord establishes their steps." —Proverbs 16:9

Conclusion: Embracing Uncertainty

The risk-reward equation is at the heart of progress. Whether in personal growth, leadership, or faith, calculated risks are the bridges that carry us from where we are to where we want to be.

Taking risks is never easy, but it's essential for growth and transformation. When we approach uncertainty with wisdom, courage, and faith, we open ourselves to opportunities that can change lives—not just our own, but those of the people we lead and serve.

Remember, the greatest rewards often require the greatest leaps. So, step forward boldly. The rewards are waiting on the other side of uncertainty.

Chapter 16:
Making Peace with Imperfection

Letting Go of Perfectionism to Achieve Authentic Success

Perfection is a seductive illusion. It whispers promises of validation, acceptance, and extraordinary achievement. But behind its shimmering veil lies a trap—a relentless pursuit that often leaves us drained, disconnected, and, paradoxically, far from perfect.

In our fast-paced, comparison-driven world, perfectionism has become a badge of honor. But the truth is, striving for perfection isn't a path to success; it's often a roadblock. The key to living authentically and achieving lasting success is not in being flawless but in embracing our imperfections.

The Weight of Perfectionism

Emily Langston learned this lesson the hard way. A talented architect in her early 30s, Emily had built a reputation for designing breathtaking homes that seemed plucked from dreams. She was meticulous, detail-oriented, and unwilling to compromise. Her colleagues admired her commitment, but behind closed doors, Emily was unraveling.

Her quest for perfection turned even the smallest project into a monumental task. Every sketch had to be reworked until it was "just right," every meeting meticulously rehearsed. While her clients were dazzled by the results, Emily was burning out. She avoided risks, fearing even the slightest mistake would tarnish her reputation.

One sleepless night, as she poured over blueprints for a high-profile client, Emily reached a breaking point. Exhausted, she stared at a design she'd revised for the sixth time and muttered, "What am I doing this for?" It was a question she'd been too scared to ask herself before.

The Myth of Flawlessness

The perfectionist mindset convinces us that success depends on never failing, never stumbling, and never showing weakness. But this is a myth. True success—authentic success—doesn't come from flawless execution; it comes from courage, vulnerability, and resilience.

In her moment of clarity, Emily began to reevaluate what success meant to her. She realized that her most celebrated designs weren't born from perfection but from experimentation and risk-taking. Some of her greatest breakthroughs had stemmed from happy accidents and bold choices, not painstakingly crafted plans.

Embracing Imperfection

To embrace imperfection is not to settle for mediocrity; it's to recognize that imperfection is what makes us human. The cracks in our plans, the flaws in our work—these are where creativity and authenticity seep in.

Emily decided to challenge her perfectionism. She started by giving herself permission to submit her first draft instead of endlessly revising it. She set boundaries on how much time she'd spend obsessing over details. Most importantly, she began to celebrate progress instead of punishing herself for perceived shortcomings.

The results were transformative. Emily rediscovered the joy of her craft. Her designs became bolder, more innovative. She collaborated more freely with her team, unafraid to share incomplete ideas. Her work didn't suffer; it thrived.

Strategies for Letting Go

If you've spent years chasing perfection, breaking free from its grip can feel daunting. Here are some strategies to help you start:

1. Redefine Success

Ask yourself what truly matters to you. Is it accolades and approval, or is it creating meaningful work and living a fulfilling life? By focusing on what's authentic to you, you can let go of the unrealistic standards that perfectionism imposes.

2. Set "Good Enough" Goals

Not every task needs to be a masterpiece. Learn to differentiate between what requires excellence and what simply needs to get done. Aim for progress over perfection.

3. Celebrate Failures

Shift your mindset to see failures as opportunities for growth. Each misstep brings valuable lessons that can guide you toward better results in the future.

4. Practice Self-Compassion

Treat yourself as you would a friend. When you fall short, instead of criticizing yourself, offer words of encouragement. Remember, self-compassion fuels resilience and creativity.

5. Surround Yourself with Support

Share your struggles with trusted friends or mentors. Often, they can offer perspective and remind you that imperfections are not weaknesses—they're part of the process.

The Beauty of Authentic Success

Emily's story is not unique. Every person who achieves authentic success must grapple with imperfection. Whether you're an artist, entrepreneur, or parent, the journey to fulfillment is rarely neat and linear. But it is real.

Perfectionism keeps us in a constant state of "not enough"—not good enough, not ready enough, not worthy enough. But when we embrace imperfection, we find freedom. We discover that our flaws don't diminish us; they make us whole.

Letting go of perfectionism is not about lowering your standards. It's about redefining them. Success isn't about being flawless; it's about being authentic. And when you're authentic, you're unstoppable.

As Emily now tells her clients, "A perfect house is lifeless. It's the imperfections—the hand-carved table with a crack, the asymmetrical garden path—that make a home feel alive." The same is true for you. Embrace your imperfections, and watch your life transform into something far more extraordinary than perfect—it will be real.

Chapter 17:
The Spirit of a Conqueror

"It is not the fall that defines you, but the decision to rise."

Every great conqueror throughout history has faced defeat. Alexander the Great, Napoleon, Mandela—none were strangers to setbacks. What made them legendary was not their immunity to failure but their unwavering spirit to overcome. To be a conqueror is not about a life devoid of struggle; it is about summoning the courage to press on despite it.

The Battle Within

Before we can conquer the external challenges of life, we must face the battles within ourselves. Doubt, fear, and insecurity often roar louder than any external obstacle. They whisper lies that tell us, "You're not good enough," or "You've failed too many times to succeed now."

But here is the truth: Those whispers are not your reality. They are merely the echoes of your past experiences, not the voice of your potential. You are stronger than your fears, wiser than your mistakes, and braver than you realize.

Victory Through Perseverance

Think of a seed buried in the soil. In darkness, it struggles to push through the dirt, breaking apart to find the light. The process is grueling, but the seed persists, knowing that its purpose is not in staying buried but in blooming.

You are that seed. Life may bury you in circumstances that feel overwhelming, but your ability to persevere will bring you to the surface.

Conqueror's Affirmations:
- "I am not defined by my failures; I am refined by them."
- "I rise because my purpose is greater than my pain."
- "Every setback is a setup for my greatest comeback."

When life feels heavy, remember that even the darkest night gives way to dawn. You were born to be a conqueror, to face adversity head-on, and to turn every misstep into a stepping stone toward mastery.

Chapter 18:
A New Kind of Hope

"Hope isn't just wishful thinking—it's a declaration that tomorrow can be better, even when today feels impossible."

Hope is a fragile thing, especially when life has beaten you down. It's easy to lose sight of it when your circumstances scream failure, rejection, and despair. But I learned that hope isn't about what you see—it's about what you believe.

And belief, as I discovered, is a choice.

The Weight of the Past

Even as I began to rebuild my life, the weight of my past threatened to drag me down. There were moments when I couldn't look in the mirror without seeing my failures staring back at me.

The enemy loves to remind you of what you've lost, of where you've been. He whispers, *You're not good enough. You'll never make it.*

But then I'd remember Lamentations 3:22-23:

"Because of the Lord's great love, we are not consumed, for His compassions never fail. They are new every morning; great is Your faithfulness."

That verse became my lifeline. Every morning, I told myself: *Today is a new day. His mercies are new. I don't have to be defined by yesterday.*

Small Steps Forward

Hope doesn't come all at once. It comes in small, quiet steps.

For me, it started with the simple act of getting up each day and choosing to believe that God still had a plan for me. I found a job, saved what little I could, and slowly started to rebuild.

There were setbacks, of course. Times when I felt like giving up. But every time I stumbled, God reminded me, *You're not walking this road alone.*

A Community of Believers

One of the greatest gifts God gave me during this time was a community of people who believed in me when I couldn't believe in myself.

My parents, Siblings and aunts and uncles They didn't care about my past—they cared about my future. They encouraged me, prayed with me, and reminded me that I was still worthy of love and purpose.

Their kindness gave me hope. It showed me that God often works through people to bring His light into our darkest moments.

The Power of Giving Back

As I began to heal, I realized that hope isn't something you keep to yourself—it's something you give away.

I started volunteering at shelters, sharing my story with people who were where I had been. I told them, "I know it's hard. I know it feels impossible. But I'm standing here as proof that God can bring beauty from ashes."

Helping others gave me a new sense of purpose. It reminded me that even in my brokenness, I could still make a difference.

Hope in Action

One day, a young man approached me after I spoke at a community center. He was homeless, jobless, and ready to give up. "How did you do it?" he asked. "How did you keep going?"

I looked him in the eyes and said, "I didn't. God did. I just trusted Him to carry me when I couldn't carry myself."

I shared with him one of my favorite quotes:

"When you reach the end of your rope, tie a knot and hang on."
– Franklin D. Roosevelt

He nodded, tears in his eyes. "I think I can do that," he said.

And that's the thing about hope—it's contagious.

A New Perspective

Hope doesn't mean life will suddenly be easy. It doesn't mean you'll never face challenges again. But it does mean you can face them with the assurance that God is with you, that better days are ahead, and that you are stronger than you think.

Romans 5:3-5 says, *"We also glory in our sufferings, because we know that suffering produces perseverance; perseverance, character; and character, hope. And hope does not put us to shame, because God's love has been poured out into our hearts."*

That verse became my anthem. It reminded me that every trial I faced had a purpose, and that purpose was to build something unshakable within me.

Living with Hope

Hope became my fuel. It gave me the strength to keep moving forward, to dream again, to believe that my story wasn't over.

And as I stood on the other side of rock bottom, I realized something profound:

Hope isn't about avoiding the storms—it's about knowing the sun will shine again.

Chapter 19:
Teaching Others to Fail Forward

Helping Those Around You Embrace Failure as a Stepping Stone to Mastery

There's a quote that often floats around in self-help circles: "You are the average of the five people you spend the most time with." While this might sound like a nice piece of motivational rhetoric, it actually holds more truth than we care to admit. The people you surround yourself with have a direct impact on your attitude, your mindset, and—yes—your relationship with failure.

If you've embraced the fail-forward mentality and learned to see failure as a stepping stone to mastery, then the next step in your growth is sharing that mindset with others. Because let's be real: you can't build a strong foundation of success if the people around you are constantly trying to avoid failure like it's the plague.

Teaching others to fail forward is one of the most rewarding (and challenging) things you can do. It requires patience, empathy, and a willingness to let others stumble and fall—not because you want them to fail, but because you know that, in the long run, those stumbles are the fastest way to learn and grow.

The Trap of "Perfectionism"

One of the hardest truths to accept is that perfectionism is not the path to success—it's the path to stagnation. And if you've spent enough time with people who are obsessed with getting things "right" the first time, you'll see it all too clearly. They're afraid to take risks, to experiment, and ultimately, to fail. They'd rather stick with what they know than venture into the unknown. But this mindset doesn't just limit them—it limits everyone they interact with.

Think about the times you've worked with someone who has been paralyzed by the fear of doing something wrong. It's exhausting, isn't it? There's no energy to move forward, no momentum, no creativity. In fact, it often feels like you're walking on eggshells just to keep them from feeling like they've failed.

The reality is, perfectionism is a barrier. It's a way of playing small. But when you teach others how to fail forward, you're teaching them that it's okay to fall. It's okay to screw up. It's okay to mess things up—because that's the way forward. When you fail, you grow. When you grow, you succeed. Simple as that.

Starting with Yourself: Modeling the Fail-Forward Mindset

Before you can encourage others to fail forward, you have to model it. And let's face it: this is the hard part. It's one thing to talk about embracing failure; it's another to live it out in front of others.

But if you can't take risks yourself, how can you expect anyone else to? If you avoid the hard conversations, if you hesitate to try new things because you're afraid of failure, how can you teach others that failure is a part of the journey? If you want others to learn to fail forward, you first have to embody it.

For instance, when was the last time you showed vulnerability in front of others? When did you admit that you tried something, and it didn't go as planned? It doesn't matter if it's at work, with your friends, or at home—being transparent about your own failures allows the people around you to see that it's okay to stumble. By doing this, you're giving them permission to fail as well.

There's no "perfect" way to live or work—there's only progress. And when you share your setbacks, your growth, and your mistakes with others, you're setting a powerful example. You're showing that it's possible to keep going, even when things aren't going according to plan. And you're helping them see that failure isn't the enemy—it's a vital part of success.

Helping Others Redefine Failure

One of the hardest aspects of teaching others to fail forward is helping them redefine what failure means. To many, failure is synonymous with giving up, not being good enough, or falling short. But you and I both know that failure is nothing more than a stepping stone toward success.

When you mentor someone or guide them through a process, it's vital to help them shift their perspective on failure. Instead of fearing it, encourage them to embrace it. Help them understand that failure is not a personal indictment on their abilities—it's feedback. It's a lesson in disguise.

For example, if a colleague misses a major deadline, instead of offering them a simple "it's okay" or "better luck next time," ask questions like, "What do you think went wrong?" or "What can we learn from this?" Encourage them to analyze the situation, identify the areas for growth, and adjust their approach moving forward.

This doesn't mean you should minimize their disappointment or brush off their feelings. It simply means shifting the focus from the failure itself to the lesson it offers. In doing so, you help them see that their mistakes are not the end of the world, but a valuable part of their development. You're teaching them how to fail forward.

The Power of a Growth Mindset

One of the most powerful ways to help others embrace failure is to instill in them a growth mindset. A growth mindset is the belief that skills and intelligence can be developed through dedication, hard work, and learning from mistakes. This mindset is the backbone of failure-forward thinking.

You've probably heard of Carol Dweck's research on growth versus fixed mindsets. People with a fixed mindset believe their abilities are static—they either have talent or they don't. People with a growth mindset, on the other hand, believe that with effort and perseverance, they can improve and develop new skills.

When you encourage others to embrace a growth mindset, you empower them to see failure as a natural part of their development. Instead of viewing challenges as threats to their identity or abilities, they start to view them as opportunities to learn and grow.

If you notice a colleague struggling with a task, or if a friend feels stuck in their career, ask them questions that promote a growth mindset:

- "What could you try differently next time?"
- "What did you learn from this experience?"
- "What small steps could you take to improve?"

By encouraging reflection and focusing on the process of learning, you help others build resilience. You help them see that failure doesn't define them—it refines them. And with each setback, they become more capable and more confident.

Creating a Safe Space for Failure

It's one thing to preach about the power of failure—it's another to create an environment where people actually feel safe to fail. If you want to truly teach others to fail forward, you need to create a culture where mistakes are not met with judgment, shame, or blame.

This starts with fostering an atmosphere of psychological safety. People need to feel that they can try, fail, and learn without the fear of being ridiculed or penalized. They need to know that their mistakes won't be held against them forever, and that they'll have the support they need to bounce back.

Think about the best teams you've been a part of. What made them successful? Chances are, it was a shared belief that failure was part of the process. In those environments, you weren't afraid to speak up, to experiment, or to take risks. That sense of safety and support is what allows people to fail forward with confidence.

Empowering Others to Lead

Finally, teaching others to fail forward isn't just about being their guide—it's about empowering them to be leaders of their own growth. Once people understand the value of failure and embrace it as a tool for mastery, they'll take ownership of their learning and their journey.

Encourage others to share their failures, their lessons, and their growth with others. As they learn to navigate their setbacks and master the art of failure-forward thinking, they'll begin to pass on this knowledge to others, creating a ripple effect of growth, resilience, and empowerment.

The truth is, when you teach someone to fail forward, you're not just helping them recover from mistakes. You're giving them the tools to lead, to innovate, and to create a legacy of mastery.

Conclusion: A Legacy of Growth

Teaching others to fail forward is not just about fixing their mistakes—it's about helping them develop a mindset that will serve them for a lifetime. By modeling failure as a tool for growth, by helping them redefine failure, and by fostering a culture of psychological safety, you're setting them on a path to greater success, no matter what challenges they face.

In the end, success is not about avoiding failure. It's about how we respond to it. And if you can teach others to respond with resilience, curiosity, and perseverance, you'll have helped them build not just a career, but a life of mastery.

And that's the kind of legacy that lasts.

Chapter 20:
The Sweet Spot of Success

Celebrating Milestones and Reflecting on How Failure Paved the Way

Success. It's a word we all crave, a destination that seems just out of reach, yet constantly pulling us forward. When you finally reach that moment—whether it's launching a business, landing a job, mending a broken relationship, or simply achieving a long-sought goal—there's an undeniable sweetness to it. Success feels like standing on top of a mountain, looking at the view below, and knowing you've made it. But here's the catch: to truly savor the sweetness of success, you have to first acknowledge the bitter taste of failure that came before it.

And, more importantly, you have to celebrate the milestones along the way that led you to that moment of triumph. Because let's be honest—success doesn't happen overnight. It's the culmination of small, hard-won victories, setbacks, mistakes, and lessons learned. And while the moment you finally reach your goal may feel like an arrival, it's actually the end of one chapter and the start of another. The real question is: how do we celebrate these milestones while reflecting on the failures that got us there?

The Elusive Sweet Spot

What does success really feel like? Often, when we think of success, we imagine an end goal: the promotion, the big paycheck, the perfect relationship, the dream house. These are the moments we picture when we think about achieving something significant.

But when you look at success through the lens of someone who has failed, you begin to see that it's not just about the destination—it's about the journey.

The sweet spot of success exists in the space between failure and triumph, where hard work, learning, and growth intersect. It's the realization that failure isn't something to be ashamed of or hidden away. Instead, it's woven into the fabric of your success story, giving it depth, texture, and authenticity. It's this recognition that makes success not just sweeter, but more meaningful.

You see, if you're always chasing the perfect moment—the day everything aligns and you can finally say, "I've made it"—you'll miss the quiet, powerful moments that really matter. These are the moments when you reflect on the times you almost gave up, the times you doubted yourself, the times you got knocked down, but still kept going. These moments of reflection are not just the starting point of success—they are the success itself. The sweet spot is in the becoming, not the being.

Celebrating the Small Wins

I'll be the first to admit: I'm a bit of a workaholic. When I reach a milestone, I tend to move quickly to the next project. I get so focused on what's ahead that I forget to celebrate what I've already accomplished. But here's the thing: milestones matter. They're the proof that you've grown, that you've learned, and that you're capable of more than you ever thought possible.

Take a moment to look back at where you started. Think about the small victories that led to the larger ones. Maybe you nailed a tough presentation, took a risk that paid off, or finally managed to get your sleep schedule in check after months of chaos. These small wins are stepping stones. They add up. And even though they might not feel as monumental as the bigger goals, they carry just as much weight in the journey of success.

The real question is: how can we celebrate these small wins in a way that makes us feel proud, without waiting for the big, flashy moments? How can we create habits of appreciation and acknowledgment?

1. Take a Moment to Reflect

Pause and give yourself credit. Too often, we rush through life without taking a breath to appreciate where we are. But reflection is key to appreciating how far you've come. Take a few minutes at the end of each week, month, or project to sit back and think about what you have achieved.

2. Mark the Occasion

Whether it is a small personal victory or a huge professional win, don't underestimate the power of marking the occasion. Treat yourself to a small reward. Maybe it's a nice meal, a weekend getaway, or simply a quiet evening to reflect. Celebrate your wins, no matter how small they seem.

3. Share with Others

Success, big or small, is always sweeter when shared. Tell someone about the progress you have made. Sharing your milestones helps reinforce the sense of accomplishment. It also spreads the positivity to others, encouraging them to celebrate their wins as well.

The Role of Failure in Success

While we are on the topic of celebration, let us address the elephant in the room: failure. It can be tempting to want to forget about the failures that led you here, especially when you are basking in the sweet satisfaction of success. But here is the catch: failure is an inseparable part of success. Without failure, success would have no meaning.

Failure gives success its flavor. Think about it: every failure teaches you something that pushes you one step closer to your goals. Without failure, you would not learn to persevere, innovate, or adapt. It is like a recipe—too much of one ingredient can spoil the dish, but a balanced mix of flavors creates something amazing.

Reflecting on failure does not mean dwelling in the past or beating yourself up for mistakes made. It means recognizing the value of what went wrong and understanding how it shaped what went right. For instance, when I look back on my first business venture that failed, I do not see it as a wasted effort. Instead, I see it as a priceless teacher. That failure showed me what I was truly capable of, it taught me the importance of resilience, and it helped me develop the mindset needed to succeed in future endeavors.

Now, every time I face a new challenge, I carry those lessons with me. The failures do not feel like setbacks—they feel like building blocks. And when I reach a milestone, I celebrate not just the success itself, but the failures that got me there.

How Failure Refines Success

We tend to think of success as a momentary victory, but real success is about long-term growth. The best things in life take time to develop, and failure is the crucible where that development happens. Without failure, success would lack depth and context. It would be like a shiny, untested object that is pretty to look at but fragile when you try to hold it.

Each failure teaches you resilience, adaptability, and resourcefulness. It pushes you to rethink your approach, to innovate, to stretch your limits. Success, then, is not a line we cross at a particular point in time, but a continuous journey of learning and growing.

Think of failure as a sculptor shaping a block of marble. The sculptor chips away at the stone, sometimes making mistakes, but each strike gets the piece closer to the final masterpiece. Your failures are like those chiseled marks—they may feel painful at the time, but they create something beautiful in the end.

The Power of Gratitude

One of the most powerful ways to enjoy the sweet spot of success is to cultivate gratitude. Gratitude does not just help you appreciate the good things in life—it also helps you find value in the struggles and setbacks. By acknowledging both your wins and losses with gratitude, you create a deeper sense of fulfillment.

When you are in the sweet spot of success, it is easy to get caught up in the excitement of what's to come. But taking a step back and recognizing all that you have overcome helps keep you grounded. It reminds you that success is not about the destination—it is about how you got there.

Reflecting and Moving Forward

As you reach your milestones, take the time to reflect on what you have learned from both your successes and your failures. Success is not a destination—it is a continual process. The sweet spot is a place where you can savor your accomplishments without losing sight of the journey. It is a moment of clarity where you realize that each step, no matter how small or imperfect, has been a vital part of your story.

So, celebrate. Celebrate the victories, the lessons, the failures, and the growth. Acknowledge the arduous work, the late nights, the sacrifices. But remember: the sweet spot of success is not just about where you have been—it is about where you are going. And if you keep learning, growing, and embracing the journey, the sweetness will never fade.

Chapter 21:
Helping Hands, Healing Hearts

"Service to others is the rent we pay for the privilege of living on this earth." – Muhammad Ali

As I rebuilt my life, something unexpected happened. God turned my focus outward. He showed me that my pain wasn't just about me—it was a tool, a bridge to connect with others who were hurting.

In the process of helping others, I found healing for myself.

A Broken Man Meets Broken People

When you've been broken, you recognize the same cracks in others. You see it in their eyes, the way they avoid direct conversation, the way their shoulders slump like the weight of the world is pressing them down.

At shelters and community centers, I met men and women who had lost everything—just like I had. They carried the same shame, the same fear, the same emptiness.

But I also saw something else in them: potential.

One Small Act of Kindness

One day, while volunteering at a local shelter, I met a young man named Derrick. He was only 20 but looked like life had aged him beyond his years.

"I'm done," he said, sitting on a bench outside the shelter. "I can't keep doing this."

I sat next to him and listened as he poured out his story. Abandonment. Addiction. Hopelessness.

When he finished, I said, "Derrick, I've been where you are. I know what it feels like to want to give up. But let me tell you something: you're still here. That means God isn't done with you yet."

I gave him my number and told him to call me anytime. Over the next few weeks, we talked often, and I shared my story with him.

One day, he walked into church, sat in the back row, and cried through the entire service. Afterward, he told me, "I want what you have—peace."

That moment wasn't just about him—it was about God reminding me of the power of showing up for someone else.

The Joy of Serving

Helping others doesn't require a big stage or a perfect life. Sometimes, it's as simple as being present, listening, or offering a word of encouragement.

I started organizing food drives, leading Bible studies, and mentoring young men who had fallen through the cracks of society. It wasn't always easy—some people pushed me away or didn't want my help. But for every rejection, there was a breakthrough.

Lessons in Compassion

One of the most profound lessons I learned was that compassion is a choice. It's choosing to see people not as they are, but as they could be.

Jesus modeled this perfectly. He didn't avoid the broken or the outcasts—He sought them out. He touched lepers, dined with sinners, and offered grace to those who felt unworthy.

I tried to follow His example, even when it was uncomfortable.

No One There for Me

For every person I helped, there were moments when I wished someone would do the same for me. It was hard, pouring out for others while feeling empty myself.

But then I realized something: God was my source. He was filling me up so I could pour into others.

Isaiah 58:10 says, *"If you spend yourselves in behalf of the hungry and satisfy the needs of the oppressed, then your light will rise in the darkness, and your night will become like the noonday."*

That verse became a promise I clung to.

Building Something Bigger

Over time, I realized that helping others wasn't just about meeting immediate needs—it was about building something lasting.

I started working with local organizations to create programs for at-risk youth. We offered job training, mentorship, and a safe space for them to share their struggles.

Every success story felt like a victory—not just for them, but for God's kingdom.

Helping Others, Healing Myself

There's a strange thing that happens when you serve others: you start to heal, too.

In pouring into others, I found new purpose. In sharing my story, I found my voice. In loving the broken, I learned to love myself again.

Helping others reminded me that my life mattered, that my struggles weren't wasted, and that God could use even the worst parts of my story for good.

A Ripple Effect

I'll never forget the day Derrick, the young man I mentored, stood up in church and shared his testimony.

"I was lost," he said, his voice shaking. "But God sent someone to remind me that I wasn't forgotten."

As he spoke, I realized that every act of kindness, every word of encouragement, creates a ripple effect. The impact goes far beyond what we can see.

A Life of Service

I made a decision that day: I would dedicate the rest of my life to helping others. Because when you've been given a second chance, the best way to honor it is to pay it forward.

And in the process, you might just find that the hands you extend to others are the same hands that lift you up.

Chapter 22:
Failing in Relationships and Life

Applying the Principles of Failing Forward to Personal and Professional Relationships

When we talk about failure, our minds often jump to business ventures, career goals, or personal achievements. But some of the hardest failures to navigate are the ones that hit closest to home—those in our relationships. Whether it's a romantic partnership, a friendship, or a professional connection, the pain of failure in relationships is uniquely raw.

It's easy to believe that the people in our lives should "get us," that we should be able to love, communicate, and support each other effortlessly. We look around at the seemingly perfect relationships—on social media, in movies, in the lives of others—and feel like we're falling short.

But the truth is, relationships are complicated. They require vulnerability, patience, forgiveness, and growth. And sometimes, despite our best efforts, they don't work out the way we want. The good news is that just like in business or personal growth, we can apply the "fail-forward" mindset to relationships—turning our setbacks into opportunities to learn, grow, and build deeper connections.

A Relationship That Fell Apart

Sophie Martinez thought she had it all figured out. At 30, she had a flourishing career as a graphic designer, a close-knit group of friends, and a relationship that seemed like it was heading toward forever. She and her partner, Josh, had been dating for over three years. They had big dreams of building a life together—traveling, buying a home, maybe even starting a family.

But as the months went by, cracks began to form in their connection. Sophie became increasingly frustrated with Josh's inability to communicate his feelings. Josh, in turn, felt smothered by Sophie's need for constant reassurance. They fought more often, but neither of them knew how to bridge the growing divide between them.

Then, one afternoon, Josh told Sophie that he was unsure about their future. It felt like the floor had been ripped out from under her. She wasn't ready to let go, but Josh had made up his mind. The breakup was devastating, not just because of the loss of the relationship, but because Sophie felt like she had failed. Failed in her ability to love, to communicate, and to hold on to what she thought was the perfect future.

For weeks, Sophie replayed every conversation, every moment where things went wrong. She blamed herself for not seeing the warning signs, for not fixing things when she could. But over time, she came to realize something crucial: failure in relationships wasn't about losing, it was about learning.

The Fail-Forward Mindset in Relationships

Just like any other area of life, relationships don't always unfold according to plan. We can't predict how people will behave, how emotions will evolve, or how external factors will affect our connections. What we can control, however, is how we respond to the challenges and failures that arise.

The fail-forward mindset teaches us that failure isn't a defeat; it's a stepping stone toward personal growth and deeper understanding. In relationships, this mindset means embracing mistakes as learning opportunities, letting go of perfection, and staying open to change and improvement.

When Sophie reflected on her relationship with Josh, she didn't just focus on what went wrong. She thought about what she had learned.

"I realized that I hadn't communicated my needs as clearly as I thought I had," Sophie said in a conversation with a close friend a few months later. "I was so focused on making him feel loved and appreciated that I didn't take the time to listen to his concerns. I wasn't perfect, but I'm learning to be a better listener, a better partner."

Sophie understood that the failure of her relationship wasn't a reflection of her inability to love or her worth as a person. It was a signal that there were areas she could improve in—communication, self-awareness, and emotional honesty. The failure didn't define her; it refined her.

Learning from Our Mistakes

In every failed relationship—whether personal or professional—there are valuable lessons to be learned. And while it may hurt, the process of learning from those mistakes can shape us into better versions of ourselves. Here are some principles to apply when you face failure in relationships:

1. Failure Is a Learning Opportunity, Not a Character Defect

It's easy to fall into the trap of believing that a failed relationship means you are unworthy of love or connection. But failure is not a reflection of your value. It's simply a moment where something didn't work out as planned. Instead of viewing it as a personal shortcoming, ask yourself, "What can I learn from this experience?" This mindset shift helps you grow, not shrink.

2. Embrace Vulnerability

Often, the reason relationships falter is because we're afraid to be vulnerable. We hide parts of ourselves, unwilling to risk rejection or discomfort. But vulnerability is the cornerstone of authentic connection. It's through being open, honest, and raw that we create the space for deeper understanding and growth—both in ourselves and with others.

3. Communicate with Clarity

Misunderstandings are often at the root of relationship breakdowns. Learning how to communicate effectively—expressing your feelings, listening actively, and understanding the needs of others—can prevent many issues from escalating. When Sophie realized her communication gap with Josh, it became a turning point in how she approached relationships going forward.

4. Practice Self-Forgiveness

In relationships, it's easy to fall into a pattern of self-blame. You think about all the things you could have done differently, all the chances you missed. But it's essential to forgive yourself. No one is perfect, and relationships are a two-way street. You can learn from your mistakes without carrying the burden of guilt. Be kind to yourself, and allow yourself the grace to grow.

5. Resilience Is Key

Relationships are messy. They require resilience—the ability to bounce back from disappointments, misunderstandings, and pain.

Life will throw curveballs, but those who succeed in relationships are the ones who keep trying. They remain open to love, to connection, and to the possibility of new beginnings.

6. Take Time to Heal

After any emotional setback, especially in relationships, healing is crucial. You can't move forward if you're still carrying the weight of the past. Take time for yourself. Rediscover your passions, focus on your personal growth, and rebuild your emotional strength. Only then can you approach future relationships with a clearer perspective and a stronger heart.

Moving Forward, Together

Sophie eventually found love again, but it was different this time. She had learned to listen, to communicate more clearly, and to be more honest about her needs. She had also learned the importance of understanding her partner's perspective and allowing space for growth within the relationship.

The failure with Josh didn't mean Sophie was destined to fail again. It meant she had grown, learned, and evolved. She had failed forward.

In both personal and professional relationships, we'll face challenges. Sometimes things will fall apart, and we'll wonder if we're cut out for love or connection. But it's not about avoiding failure—it's about using failure as a tool to get better. Every failed relationship teaches us something valuable, whether it's about the other person or about ourselves.

We cannot control everything, and not every relationship will work out. But if we embrace the fail-forward mindset, we can move forward, each time a little wiser, a little stronger, and with the heart open to the beauty of new connections.

In the end, it's not about avoiding failure, but about learning to fail forward. And when you do, you'll realize that every failure brings you one step closer to the relationships and life you've always wanted.

Chapter 23:
The Fail-Forward Mindset

Adopting a Lifelong Approach to Learning, Growth, and Resilience

Failure. It's a word we fear, avoid, and sometimes even redefine to keep from acknowledging its true power. But what if failure wasn't something to be feared at all? What if it was a necessary step toward growth, a lesson that could shape us into the people we're meant to become?

The "fail-forward" mindset invites us to look at failure differently—not as a setback, but as a springboard. It teaches us to fail with purpose, to fail with grace, and ultimately, to fail our way forward. It's about viewing every stumble not as the end of the road but as part of the journey.

Redefining Failure

For years, Jake Harrison thought failure was the worst thing that could happen to him. As the founder of a growing tech startup in New York City, Jake was driven by the desire to create something groundbreaking. But despite his passion and work ethic, his first venture ended in disaster.

The company had been his dream. He poured his soul into the project, raised capital, and assembled a talented team. But despite the hype, it quickly became clear that the product wasn't what the market wanted. The tech was promising, but the business model wasn't sustainable. Within two years, Jake had to close the doors.

In the aftermath, Jake felt devastated. He had not only lost his business but had also failed in his eyes. He took it personally. His ego was bruised, and the feeling of inadequacy lingered.

But then something unexpected happened. One evening, over drinks with an old mentor, Jake opened up about the failure. He expected sympathy, but instead, his mentor smiled and said, "Jake, you didn't fail—you're failing forward."

Jake was puzzled. "What do you mean?"

"Failure is not the end of the road," his mentor explained. "It's a detour, an opportunity to learn what works and what doesn't. The only time you truly fail is when you stop trying."

This conversation was a turning point for Jake. The idea of "failing forward" resonated deeply. He realized that every misstep had provided him with invaluable lessons. Each wrong turn had taught him more about the market, his customers, and himself than any success could have.

The Power of Failing Forward

The fail-forward mindset isn't just about learning from failure—it's about embracing failure as an essential part of the growth process. Resilience isn't built in the absence of setbacks; it's forged through them.

In fact, many of the world's most successful people have encountered failure time and time again. Thomas Edison failed thousands of times before inventing the lightbulb. J.K. Rowling faced multiple rejections before "Harry Potter" became a global phenomenon. Michael Jordan was cut from his high school basketball team, only to later become a basketball legend.

Each of these figures didn't see failure as a reason to stop; they saw it as a reason to adjust, learn, and press on. They adopted a fail-forward mindset, understanding that failure is not only inevitable but necessary for success.

Shifting Your Perspective on Failure

To truly adopt a fail-forward mindset, you must shift your perspective on what failure means. Here's how to start:

1. Embrace Failure as Part of the Process

If you're aiming for growth, failure is going to be part of the journey. Don't be discouraged by it—learn from it. When something goes wrong, ask yourself, "What can I learn from this?" This simple question turns failure into a stepping stone rather than a roadblock.

2. See Mistakes as Feedback, Not Defeat

Mistakes are not an indication of your inability; they're feedback that shows you where to adjust. When something doesn't go according to plan, take it as a signal to recalibrate. This shift in mindset will help you see mistakes as opportunities for improvement, not reasons to give up.

3. Keep the Long View

Success is rarely a straight line. It's more like a winding road full of twists, turns, and occasional dead ends. Keep your eyes on the bigger picture and remember that every setback is just a detour. Success doesn't require perfection—it requires persistence.

4. Celebrate Progress, Not Just Perfection

Instead of focusing solely on your ultimate goal, celebrate the small wins along the way. Each step forward, no matter how small, is a victory. Recognizing and appreciating these moments keeps you motivated, even when things don't go perfectly.

5. Cultivate Resilience

Resilience is the ability to bounce back after setbacks. It's about getting up, dusting yourself off, and moving forward—again and again. When you embrace failure as part of the process, you build resilience by default.

Lifelong Learning and Growth

The fail-forward mindset is not just about bouncing back from failures—it's about adopting a lifelong approach to learning and growth. In a world that is constantly changing, the ability to learn, adapt, and evolve is essential.

As you continue on your journey, remember that no one has all the answers, and no one succeeds without facing challenges. It's the people who stay curious, who remain open to learning, who keep moving forward even after failure, that ultimately succeed.

Jake's second startup was far more successful than his first. Armed with the lessons from his previous venture, he knew how to pivot when needed, adjust his approach, and stay focused on what truly mattered. His company didn't just survive; it thrived.

But it wasn't just the success that mattered to Jake—it was the mindset that had shifted. He was no longer afraid to fail. He understood that failure wasn't something to avoid; it was something to embrace, learn from, and grow through.

The Art of Failing Forward

Adopting the fail-forward mindset isn't easy. It requires a shift in how you view both yourself and the world around you. But when you embrace failure as part of the journey, it loses its power to hold you back. Instead, it becomes a tool that propels you forward.

So, the next time you fail—or when you feel like you've stumbled—don't stop. Don't retreat. Take a deep breath, ask yourself what you can learn from it, and keep moving forward. Because in the grand scheme of things, success is less about avoiding failure and more about how you respond to it.

In the end, the real failure isn't falling down—it's staying down. Keep going, keep learning, and keep failing forward. Your greatest success may just be one failure away.

Chapter 24:
The Road to Redemption

"Redemption is not just a moment, it's a journey—a long, winding road paved with grace."

Redemption doesn't happen overnight. It's not a magic wand that erases all the pain or a sudden reversal of fortune. No, redemption is a process—a step-by-step journey back to the person God always intended you to be.

For me, the road to redemption wasn't smooth. It was filled with potholes of self-doubt, detours of fear, and stretches of uncertainty. But it was also where I found God's unrelenting grace, and that made all the difference.

Step 1: Owning My Story

Before I could truly walk the path of redemption, I had to confront my past. That meant owning the choices I had made—the good, the bad, and the ugly.

One of the hardest moments came when I stood in front of a room of men at a recovery center and shared my story. I told them about my divorce, my time in jail, the nights I spent homeless, and the shame that had haunted me for years.

I expected judgment, but instead, I saw nods of understanding. One man said, "You're brave for sharing that. It gives me hope."

In that moment, I realized that owning your story isn't just about you—it's about freeing others to own theirs.

Step 2: Forgiving Myself

Forgiveness was a major milestone on my road to redemption, and the hardest person to forgive was me.

I had carried so much guilt for the mistakes I'd made, for the relationships I'd damaged, for the opportunities I'd wasted. For years, I replayed those failures in my mind, like a broken record.

But then I read Psalm 103:12:

"As far as the east is from the west, so far has He removed our transgressions from us."

If God had forgiven me, who was I to hold on to what He had already let go?

That realization was liberating. Forgiving myself didn't erase the past, but it freed me from being imprisoned by it.

Step 3: Restoring What Was Broken

Redemption also meant making amends where I could. I reached out to people I had hurt, apologized sincerely, and sought to rebuild trust.

Some relationships were restored; others weren't. But I learned that redemption isn't about the outcome—it's about the effort.

Romans 12:18 became my guide:

"If it is possible, as far as it depends on you, live at peace with everyone."

Step 4: Embracing God's Plan

As I walked this journey, I began to see how God was weaving my pain into a greater purpose. Doors opened for me to share my testimony at churches, shelters, and conferences.

Every time I stood in front of an audience, I felt a mix of fear and gratitude. Fear because I knew how raw and real my story was. Gratitude because I knew God was using it to bring hope to others.

Jeremiah 29:11 became my anthem:

"For I know the plans I have for you," declares the Lord, "plans to prosper you and not to harm you, plans to give you hope and a future."

Step 5: Walking in Grace

Redemption taught me to live in the present. Instead of dwelling on what I had lost, I started focusing on what I still had—and what I could rebuild.

Grace became my lifeline. It reminded me that I didn't have to be perfect, that I didn't have to have it all figured out. I just had to keep moving forward, one step at a time.

Funny Moments Along the Way

Redemption isn't all serious. There were plenty of moments that made me laugh, like the time I showed up to preach and realized I'd accidentally put on mismatched shoes.

"God doesn't care about your shoes," I told the congregation, grinning. "He cares about your soul."

The laughter that followed was a reminder that even on the road to redemption, it's okay to not take yourself too seriously.

A New Kind of Strength

As I continued on this journey, I discovered a strength I didn't know I had. It wasn't the kind of strength that comes from avoiding hardship—it was the kind that comes from walking through it and coming out the other side.

Nelson Mandela once said, *"The greatest glory in living lies not in never falling, but in rising every time we fall."*

Redemption is about rising—again and again and again.

The Ripple Effect of Redemption

What surprised me most about this journey was how my redemption story began to impact others. People who heard my testimony started reaching out, sharing their own struggles, and asking for guidance.

One young man told me, "Hearing your story gave me the courage to believe God can redeem mine."

That moment reminded me that redemption isn't just about what God does in your life—it's about how He uses your life to touch others.

The Ongoing Journey

The road to redemption isn't a destination; it's a lifelong journey. There are still challenges, still moments of doubt, still days when the scars of my past ache.

But every step forward reminds me of this truth: *God makes all things new.*

Revelation 21:5 says, *"Behold, I am making all things new."* That's the promise I hold onto, the light that guides me as I keep walking this road.

Chapter 25:
When You've Hit Rock Bottom

Rebuilding After Major Setbacks or Catastrophes

Let's face it: we've all been there. That moment when life seems to go off the rails, when every plan you've made seems to collapse like a deck of cards in a windstorm. Maybe you lost your job, your relationship crumbled like an overcooked cookie, or you faced a personal failure so spectacular that it made you wonder if there was some sort of cosmic "Rock Bottom" Bingo card you were unknowingly filling out.

Hitting rock bottom—however you define it—feels like getting sucker-punched by life. It's painful, disorienting, and often leaves you questioning everything. But the good news? Rock bottom is not the end. It's the start of something new. It's the foundation for rebuilding. And trust me, you'll look back one day and laugh at how bad it seemed—well, mostly.

The Day My World Fell Apart

Let me tell you a story about that moment in my life. I was 28, fresh off a failed business, still reeling from a breakup that made me question my ability to maintain any semblance of human connection, and I had just received a rejection letter from a job I thought I was perfect for. I was sitting on my couch in a haze of disbelief when my mom called. I didn't even answer; I just sent her a text that read: "I'm having a moment." She replied, "I'll bring cookies."

Now, if you've ever reached rock bottom, you know it doesn't always look like the movies. There's no dramatic music playing in the background, no slow-motion shots of you walking away from the wreckage in perfect lighting. Instead, it looks a lot like sitting on your couch in your pajamas, eating the last slice of cold pizza, and scrolling through social media while everyone else seems to have their lives together.

It was on that couch that I had the profound realization that I had no idea what I was doing. My business was a bust, my personal life was a mess, and my career aspirations? Let's just say "aspirations" were a luxury I could no longer afford. I felt like a walking disaster.

But here's the twist: I didn't stay there. At least, not forever. I realized something incredibly freeing in that moment: hitting rock bottom was just a starting point. From there, I could rebuild.

The Art of Rebuilding After a Setback

Rebuilding after hitting rock bottom is not about snapping your fingers and magically being okay. It's a process, and it requires a strategy—preferably one that doesn't involve binge-watching entire seasons of The Bachelor to avoid confronting your problems. Here's how to rise from the rubble, step by step:

1. Accept That You're Not Okay

This might sound counterintuitive, but the first step to rebuilding is acknowledging the mess. You don't have to be "fine" all the time, and it's okay to admit that you're not okay. Rock bottom is not a shameful place—it's a real, human experience. If you try to skip past the sadness, frustration, or even anger, you're just delaying the inevitable. So, grab a box of tissues (or cookies, whatever works), and let yourself feel it all.

2. Take Stock of What's Left

After everything comes crashing down, you may feel like you've lost it all. But guess what? You haven't. When I hit rock bottom, I started taking stock of the things I still had. It wasn't much, but I realized I still had a sense of humor (even if it was a little dark), a supportive family (who, as mentioned earlier, were great at showing up with cookies), and a stubborn streak that wouldn't let me give up.

Look around and find something you can cling to—whether it's a talent, a relationship, or a dream. The good news is, you always have something left to work with.

3. Start Small and Build Up

Rome wasn't built in a day, and neither is a comeback. Start with small steps. Maybe that's getting out of bed on time, returning a phone call, or signing up for a class you've been thinking about. Celebrate those little victories like they're huge. Because honestly, when you're rebuilding, every small win is a giant leap forward.

I remember when my first "step forward" was simply deciding to get dressed in something other than sweatpants. Big deal, right? But it felt like a personal victory worthy of confetti.

4. Reframe Your Mindset

Rock bottom is painful, but it's also an opportunity to shift your perspective. You can either let it crush you or you can use it as a launch pad for the next chapter. I decided that failure wasn't an end—it was a plot twist. Sure, I had to face the fact that I made some bad decisions, but it didn't mean I was doomed forever.

Reframing the narrative you tell yourself can transform the situation. Instead of, "I failed, so I'll never succeed," try "I failed, but I'm learning and growing from it." In fact, embrace failure like an old friend. The more you face setbacks head-on, the easier it is to use them as fuel for success.

5. Surround Yourself with the Right People

One of the most important steps in rebuilding is finding your tribe. It's easy to isolate yourself when things go wrong, but the people around you can be your biggest supporters or your greatest critics. Choose wisely.

When I was at my lowest, I leaned heavily on friends and family who didn't judge me for my failures but encouraged me to try again. They listened, offered perspective, and—let's be real—provided a lot of chocolate. If you can't find people who will lift you up, at least find someone who will laugh at your terrible jokes until you're able to laugh at yourself again.

6. Don't Rush the Process

There's no set timeline for rebuilding. Some days will be easier than others, and some days you'll feel like you're back at square one. And that's okay. Healing is a messy, non-linear process. It's like trying to clean up a broken vase—you pick up one piece, only to realize there's another shard you missed.

Just remember: it's okay to take your time. Be patient with yourself. If you rush the process, you'll miss out on important lessons along the way. Take the time you need to heal, learn, and grow.

7. Learn to Laugh About It

Eventually, after all the tears and self-reflection, you'll start to see the humor in your situation. You'll look back and think, "I can't believe I thought that was the end of the world." Laughter is a sign that you've moved forward, and it's an important part of the healing process.

My rock bottom is now a funny story I tell at parties. Sometimes, it feels like a lifetime ago, and I laugh at how seriously I took every single setback. That doesn't mean I'm not still working on myself, but it does mean I've learned that life doesn't have to be perfect. It just has to keep moving forward.

Rebuilding: The Best Mess You'll Ever Make

In the end, hitting rock bottom is just a starting point for something greater. It's a chance to reinvent, rebuild, and come back stronger. Sure, you might get a little dusty in the process. You'll probably make mistakes, question everything, and have moments where you think, "Why is this happening to me?"

But the beauty of rebuilding is that, with each brick you lay down, you're one step closer to the version of yourself who has survived it all—and come out on top.

So, the next time you feel like you've hit rock bottom, remember: it's not the end. It's just the beginning. And with a little humor, a lot of patience, and maybe a few cookies, you'll rebuild your life—stronger, wiser, and maybe just a little bit more relatable than you were before.

Chapter 26:
From Misstep to Mastery

"Failure is not the opposite of success; it is the foundation of it."

Mastery is not a destination but a journey paved with mistakes, lessons, and growth. Every misstep you take is not a mark of inadequacy but an opportunity to learn, adapt, and emerge stronger.

The Power of Perspective

When you encounter failure, how do you see it? Do you let it break you, or do you let it build you? Perspective is everything. You can see a closed door as a rejection, or you can see it as redirection. You can view a fall as an end, or you can see it as a chance to rise higher.

Walt Disney was fired for "lacking imagination." Oprah Winfrey was told she was "unfit for television." J.K. Rowling was rejected by multiple publishers. Their failures didn't stop them; instead, they fueled their determination. These missteps became the stepping stones that led them to mastery.

Turning Pain into Progress

Every scar tells a story of survival. Every stumble teaches balance. Every mistake carves wisdom into your soul. Your life is a masterpiece in progress, and every brushstroke—no matter how imperfect—adds depth to the bigger picture.

When you fail, don't retreat in shame. Reflect on what went wrong, refine your approach, and return with greater tenacity.

Remember, the greatest teacher is experience, and failure is one of its most valuable lessons.

Encouragement for the Journey:

- "Every failure is a bridge leading to your success."
- "You don't have to be perfect to make progress."
- "Mastery is not about never falling; it's about rising every single time."

A Vision of Mastery

Imagine yourself a year from now, five years from now. Picture the person you want to be—the skills you want to master, the dreams you want to fulfill, the life you want to live. That vision is not some distant fantasy; it is a reality waiting for your commitment and effort.

Mastery doesn't happen overnight, but it does happen one deliberate step at a time. Every time you fall and choose to rise, every time you learn from a misstep, you move closer to your goal.

Thought:

Life may throw challenges your way, but you are equipped to overcome them. You have within you the power to rise, to grow, and to achieve mastery. Believe in yourself, and let every misstep serve as a reminder that greatness is forged in the fires of persistence.

Chapter 27:
The Fail-Forward Framework

A step-by-step guide to analyze, learn from, and grow after mistakes

"The steps of a man are established by the Lord, when he delights in his way; though he fall, he shall not be cast headlong, for the Lord upholds his hand."

—Psalm 37:23-24

Failure is not the end—it is the beginning of a new path. Throughout history, some of the most successful individuals have embraced failure as a necessary step toward achieving greatness. What separates those who crumble under failure from those who rise is the ability to learn, adapt, and keep moving forward. This chapter introduces the Fail-Forward Framework, a step-by-step process to turn mistakes into momentum for growth.

Step 1: Acknowledge the Failure

"Whoever conceals their sins does not prosper, but the one who confesses and renounces them finds mercy."

—Proverbs 28:13

The first step in failing forward is to confront the reality of failure. Denial or deflection only prolongs its negative effects. Acknowledging failure requires humility and courage. It means admitting, "I made a mistake," or "This did not go as planned."

Acknowledgment is not about self-blame; it's about taking ownership. This act opens the door for reflection and learning.

Without acknowledgment, there can be no growth. Consider the story of Peter, who denied Jesus three times (Luke 22:54-62). Though his failure was devastating, his acknowledgment and repentance set the stage for his later transformation into a cornerstone of the early church.

Practical Tip: Write down what went wrong. Be specific, focusing on facts rather than emotions. For example: "I missed the deadline because I underestimated the time required," instead of, "I'm terrible at managing my work."

Step 2: Reflect Without Judgment

"Examine yourselves, to see whether you are in the faith. Test yourselves. Or do you not realize this about yourselves, that Jesus Christ is in you?"

—2 Corinthians 13:5

Reflection is essential to understand what led to the failure. This step requires objectivity and grace. Instead of judging yourself harshly, approach the situation as a detective gathering clues. Ask yourself:

- What decisions or actions led to this outcome?
- Were there external factors beyond my control?
- What did I assume that turned out to be incorrect?

Self-reflection is not about dwelling on what went wrong but uncovering insights for the future. The Apostle Paul, who once persecuted Christians, reflected deeply on his actions after his encounter with Christ on the road to Damascus (Acts 9). His reflection led to a complete transformation, demonstrating the power of thoughtful introspection.

Practical Tip: Use journaling to capture your reflections. End with a key takeaway, such as, "I need to communicate more clearly during team projects."

Step 3: Extract the Lessons

"For the righteous falls seven times and rises again, but the wicked stumble in times of calamity."

—Proverbs 24:16

Every failure carries a lesson, but it requires effort to uncover it. The key is to focus on growth rather than perfection. Ask yourself:

- What did this experience teach me about myself, others, or the situation?
- What would I do differently next time?
- How can I apply this lesson immediately?

The process of extracting lessons transforms failure from a painful event into a valuable teacher. Joseph's story in Genesis exemplifies this principle. Betrayed by his brothers and sold into slavery, Joseph faced multiple failures. Yet, he used every setback as an opportunity to grow in wisdom, leadership, and trust in God. Eventually, his lessons prepared him to save Egypt and his family during a famine (Genesis 37-50).

Practical Tip: Create a "lessons learned" list and review it before taking on similar challenges in the future.

Step 4: Create a Redemption Plan

"Commit your work to the Lord, and your plans will be established."

—Proverbs 16:3

Reflection and lessons are meaningless without action. The next step is to create a concrete plan for moving forward. A redemption plan focuses on specific, achievable steps to address the failure and build toward success.

- Set SMART goals: Goals should be Specific, Measurable, Achievable, Relevant, and Time-bound.
- Seek accountability: Share your plan with someone who can encourage and challenge you.
- Focus on small wins: Celebrate progress, no matter how minor, to rebuild confidence.

When Nehemiah set out to rebuild Jerusalem's walls after the Babylonian exile, he encountered opposition and setbacks. Yet, he crafted a clear plan, enlisted help, and remained focused on his mission (Nehemiah 2-6). His success came from his preparation, perseverance, and faith.

Practical Tip: Use a planner or digital tool to map out your redemption plan and track progress weekly.

Step 5: Reframe the Narrative

"And we know that in all things God works for the good of those who love him, who have been called according to his purpose."

—Romans 8:28

Failures can feel final, but they don't have to define you. Reframing the narrative means seeing your story in a new light—one where failure is a chapter, not the ending.

Reframing is about finding purpose in pain. It's about recognizing that even your missteps can serve a greater good. Jesus' crucifixion seemed like the ultimate failure to his disciples, yet it was the foundation for humanity's redemption (John 19-20).

Practical Tip: Write a positive statement about your experience, such as, "This failure taught me resilience and prepared me for greater challenges." Read it when you feel discouraged.

Step 6: Move Forward with Confidence

"Do not remember the former things, nor consider the things of old. Behold, I will do a new thing; now it shall spring forth; shall you not know it?"

—Isaiah 43:18-19

The final step in the Fail-Forward Framework is to let go of the past and move forward with confidence. Dwelling on mistakes prevents you from seizing new opportunities. Faith, determination, and action propel you toward growth.

Moving forward doesn't mean forgetting—it means carrying the lessons with you while leaving the pain behind. Trust that failure is part of the process and that God has a plan for your future.

Practical Tip: When facing a new challenge, remind yourself, "I have learned from my mistakes. I am better equipped now than before."

Failing Forward in Practice: A Case Study

Imagine a small business owner named James who launched a coffee shop that failed within its first year. Initially, James was devastated. But instead of giving up, he applied the Fail-Forward Framework:

1. Acknowledged the failure: He admitted that poor location choice and ineffective marketing played a role.

2. Reflected without judgment: James recognized he had underestimated competition in the area.

3. Extracted lessons: He learned the importance of market research and targeted advertising.

4. Created a redemption plan: James decided to relaunch in a new location with a robust marketing strategy.

5. Reframed the narrative: He saw the first attempt as invaluable business training.

6. Moved forward: Within two years, James' second coffee shop became a thriving community hub.

James' journey demonstrates how failure, when handled well, can lead to lasting success.

Conclusion: Embrace Failure as Growth

"But one thing I do: forgetting what lies behind and straining forward to what lies ahead, I press on toward the goal for the prize of the upward call of God in Christ Jesus."

—Philippians 3:13-14

The Fail-Forward Framework is not about avoiding failure but embracing it as a tool for growth. Mistakes are not the enemy—they are opportunities to learn, adapt, and grow stronger. By acknowledging failure, reflecting on its lessons, and taking action, you can turn setbacks into stepping stones for success.

Remember, failure is not the opposite of success—it is part of the journey. Trust in the process, and trust that every stumble brings you closer to your purpose.

Chapter 28:
Your Fail-Forward Legacy

How to inspire others by sharing your journey of turning mistakes into mastery.

I never thought I would end up here—writing these final words of this book. Not just because I once doubted my ability to do it, but because there were times in my life when I doubted I would survive at all. Rock bottom is not a place you visit; it is a place you become. For years, I was that place—lost in my mistakes, drowning in regret, and unable to see a way forward.

The irony is, it was not success that challenged me to write this book—it was failure. It was the version of me who had lost everything, sitting alone in the quiet, looking at my life and realizing, this cant be it. That voice whispered through the shame and darkness, urging me to stop hiding from my mistakes and instead turn them into a purpose that could outlive me.

Writing this book wasn't easy. Every word, every chapter was a mirror, forcing me to confront the ugliest parts of myself. But those reflections—the moments I wanted to quit, the memories that burned my soul—were also my greatest teachers. Through them, I realized that failure isn't the opposite of success. It's the foundation of it.

If you're reading this, you've already done something extraordinary: you've invested in the belief that you can be better. That matters more than you know. Because the truth is, change doesn't happen all at once. It's not a dramatic moment or a sudden shift; it's the small, persistent choices you make to fail forward—to turn the lessons from your pain into stepping stones for growth.

When I look back on my life now, I don't see just the mistakes, the heartbreaks, and the losses. I see the bridges they built to something greater. I see the opportunities I created by owning my flaws and being courageous enough to share them. I see the people who've reached out and told me, your story saved me.

That's the power of vulnerability and honesty—it connects us. It reminds us we're not alone. And when you can take your pain, your mistakes, and your regrets, and turn them into a map for someone else to find their way, you're creating something far greater than success. You're creating legacy.

This book isn't just about me. It's about you. The decisions you make after you close this chapter. The risks you take when you decide to face your own failures, own your story, and share it with the world. You don't need to write a book or give a speech to inspire others. You just need to live in a way that says, I chose better.

You see, life isn't about perfection. It's about progress. It's about showing up, even when it's messy. It's about falling, learning, and getting back up, not just for yourself but for the countless others who will see your courage and realize they can rise too.

If there's one thing I want you to take from this book, it's this: your mistakes do not define you—they refine you. They don't limit your future; they expand it. And when you use them to help someone else, you create a ripple effect that can transform lives.

I'm proof that you can go from being broken to becoming a builder. I'm proof that you can take every wrong turn, every shattered dream, and every regret, and turn it into something beautiful—not just for yourself but for others.

As I close this book, I'm reminded of a quote that guided me through the hardest moments:

"The world is full of people who need the person you've become after your struggles."

So, my challenge to you is simple: take your pain and turn it into purpose. Take your failures and turn them into lessons. And take this life—however imperfect—and make it extraordinary.

You have what it takes to leave a mark, to create a legacy that says, I turned my mess into a message, and in doing so, I changed the world.

Now it's your turn. Go write your legacy.

About the Author

W.J. was born and raised in the small, close-knit town of Hastings, where he grew up in a loving family that nurtured his optimism and passion for life. A man of many talents and boundless compassion, W.J. wears many hats: father, entrepreneur, philanthropist, pastor, musician, writer, and producer. Driven by a deep fear of God and an unwavering love for people, he has dedicated his life to uplifting others through faith, creativity, and service. His work reflects his belief in the power of resilience and the beauty of turning challenges into opportunities.

Made in the USA
Columbia, SC
26 March 2025